THE FLETCHER JONES FOUNDATION
HUMANITIES IMPRINT

The Fletcher Jones Foundation has endowed this imprint to foster innovative and enduring scholarship in the humanities.

Named in remembrance of

the onetime *Antioch Review* editor

and longtime Bay Area resident,

the Lawrence Grauman, Jr. Fund

supports books that address

a wide range of human rights,

free speech, and social justice issues.

Revolutionary Nonviolence

The publisher and the University of California Press Foundation gratefully acknowledge the generous support of the Fletcher Jones Foundation Imprint in Humanities.

The publisher and the University of California Press Foundation gratefully acknowledge the generous support of the Lawrence Grauman, Jr. Fund.

Revolutionary Nonviolence

ORGANIZING FOR FREEDOM

James M. Lawson Jr.

With Michael K. Honey and Kent Wong

Foreword by Angela Davis

⊞ UNIVERSITY OF CALIFORNIA PRESS

University of California Press
Oakland, California

© 2022 by James M. Lawson Jr., Michael K. Honey, and Kent Wong

First paperback printing 2024

Cataloging-in-Publication Data is on file at the Library of Congress.

ISBN 978-0-520-38784-3 (cloth : alk. paper)
ISBN 978-0-520-40229-4 (paperback : alk. paper)
ISBN 978-0-520-38785-0 (ebook)

Manufactured in the United States of America

33 32 31 30 29 28 27 26 25 24
10 9 8 7 6 5 4 3 2 1

Contents

Foreword by Angela Davis

Those who place contemporary events in historical perspective assist us to discover deeper meanings for the present. This is especially true of our movements for social justice. By giving us a sense of the continuum that links more recent struggles with those of the past, we acquire more complex understandings of potential future transformations and their conditions of possibility. In this sense, we are extremely fortunate, thanks to this book, to have access to the crucial insights of Rev. James Lawson. Rev. Lawson experienced and helped to shape the civil and human rights movements of the mid-twentieth century—the great nonviolent contestation of white supremacist political, economic, and social structures—and continues to be an important teacher and activist into the twenty-first century. It is particularly helpful to consider Rev. Lawson's ideas at this pivotal moment in the history of US social justice struggles, for we are currently in the process of reevaluating hegemonic theories and practices that have largely defined our efforts to dismantle racism over the last century and a half.

Rev. Lawson has always insisted on foregrounding the structural dimensions of racism and has urged us for many years to recognize what he calls "plantation capitalism." In the aftermath of the massive 2020 protests condemning the police lynching of George Floyd and the equally symbolic police murder of Breonna Taylor, along with many other instances of police violence, institutions throughout the country—and indeed, in many parts of the world—are engaged in processes designed to identify the many ways in which racism has been systemically reproduced over the last one hundred and fifty years. Rev. Lawson's teachings can bring a deeper understanding to this process. This means challenging governing ideologies that have characterized racism as a product of the defective attitudes of individuals. This means recognizing that simplistic analyses of racism inevitably lead to simplistic, ineffective solutions, such as those that have revolved around strategies of voluntary "color-evasiveness." To assume that racism would recede if only white people would learn how not to see color itself represents, as many have pointed out, the powerful reach of racist ideology. I am reminded of the response of a powerful white corporate figure who, some years ago, attempted to share with his staff his conviction that he was opposed to all forms of racism. He looked around the room and focused on the Black woman who told me the story, the one Black person in the room, and announced with passion, "I don't even see color." She then asked him, "So why are you looking directly at me, the only Black person present?"

Color-evasiveness may have been partially supplanted by diversity and inclusion strategies, but diversity and inclusion by themselves do not dislodge the structures of racism. Rev. Lawson urges us to focus on the ways that racism, sexism, and what he terms plantation capitalism—how the US treats the world as its plantation—intersect to construct violent barriers to change. Rev. Lawson argues that we are witnessing the emergence of a massive twenty-first-century movement that has the potential of expanding democracy, economically, politically, and socially. Unlike those who call for structural change but refuse to acknowledge the role that capitalism plays in embedding racism within social structures, he urges us to embrace strategies of intersectionality and to always remember that a nonviolent society can never be created with violent means.

Rev. Lawson worked closely with Dr. Martin Luther King Jr. and taught nonviolence organizing and philosophy in many of the movements of the 1960s. He taught first principles to the Little Rock Nine high school students, John Lewis, C. T. Vivian, Diane Nash, and others who formed the core of the early sit-in movement and freedom rides to desegregate public accommodations in the South. He was one of the founders of the Student Nonviolent Coordinating Committee and led the strategy committee for the Memphis sanitation strike in 1968, when an assassin took Dr. King's life. Rev. Lawson went on to promote nonviolent direct action in Los Angeles and across the country, supporting labor rights and immigrant rights and an end to imperialism and plantation capitalism. Now in his nineties, he has retained and expanded his radicalism, and his words are more important than ever.

Angela Y. Davis
Distinguished Professor Emerita
History of Consciousness and Feminist Studies
University of California, Santa Cruz

Preface

Much of this book is made up of transcripts of talks by Rev. Lawson and interviews with him. We have edited these (with his permission) much as if they were an oral history, moving a few paragraphs around to make it easier to read in sequence, with minimal copyediting. To hear and see Rev. Lawson speak is to experience the power of the prophetic tradition in the African American church. Using few if any notes, Lawson in person provides an exceptionally compelling oral presentation. Though we cannot replicate that experience here, readers can get a sense of his speaking style and his analysis.

There are many other sources of Rev. Lawson's talks and writings about him online and in print, and some are listed at the end of this book. We do not offer a broad bibliography, however, but instead focus on a few sources that can help put Rev. Lawson's life and work into context. We encourage readers to explore the vast and exciting literature on freedom and nonviolence movements for social change.

We hope this collection can help new generations in the struggle to overturn forces of systemic violence through ordinary people's power based on the principles of love and solidarity. No matter who or where you are, no matter your race, ethnicity, class, gender, nationality, or religion, you can use nonviolent action to struggle for justice and peace. You too can help transform society without inflicting more harm, to help us reach new frontiers of the beloved community. You too can build toward a moral revolution.

We wish to thank the following individuals for their hard work in making this publication possible. At the UCLA Labor Center, Julie Monroe provided outstanding aid in editing, obtaining photo permissions, and conscientiously guiding the entire process to publication. Also at the UCLA Labor Center, graduate student researchers Brittnee Meitzenheimer and Domale Keys assisted with editing, and Lily Hernandez and Kandice Rander helped in locating the photos and artwork. At the University of Washington, Tacoma, Victoria Ahrens transcribed the recordings of Rev. Lawson's Tacoma 2008 lectures; Paul Lovelady and his crew in the media office filmed Rev. Lawson's talks; Adam Nolan provided research for the film *Love and Solidarity: Rev. James Lawson and Nonviolence in the Search for Workers' Rights*, and Lucas Dambergs organized Rev. Lawson's film interviews, which we have drawn on for this book; Casey Reynolds Wagner located photos and provided technology assistance; and Kyle Veldhuizen created and maintains the website supporting Lawson film materials at loveandsolidarity .com. The Radcliffe Institute for Advanced Research at Harvard provided support for Michael Honey's work and supported the work of research partner Ria Modak, who provided reading and editing assistance.

Special thanks to Dennis C. Dickerson, the James J. Lawson Jr. Professor of History at Vanderbilt University; to Professor Clayborn Carson at Stanford University; and to anonymous readers at the University of California Press for their thoughts and suggestions.

Thanks also to scholar and activist Mary Elizabeth King at the James Lawson Institute and to the Martin Luther King Jr. Research and Education Institute at Stanford University for providing invaluable resources and inspiration in continuing the teaching and practice of nonviolent struggle.

Michael K. Honey
Haley Professor of Humanities,
University of Washington, Tacoma

Kent Wong
Director, University of California
Los Angeles Labor Center

Introduction to James M. Lawson's Talks, Dialogues, and Interviews

MICHAEL K. HONEY

Today we confront some of the gravest challenges in human history. People all over the world calling for democratic freedom, self-determination, and planetary survival are challenging systems of violence and oppression. Can we do more? Can we be more effective? Can we bring about radical change without increasing violence? James M. Lawson, one of the great teachers of nonviolence, says yes. According to him, life's "cruelty systems" can be overcome by "a force more powerful." Nonviolence, he says, provides the greatest power to transform human relations for the better, if we know how to use it.[1]

Many people do not understand nonviolence, even though people following its principles and practices have built many successful movements: nonviolence has helped to bring down racial apartheid, end military and police violence, close prisons, and overthrow dictatorships. This book distills Lawson's classic teachings on how to use the principles, history, and practice of nonviolence to pragmatically organize for change. His insights remain fresh because they are relevant to today's movements for democracy, human rights, and liberation.

Many people do not know Lawson's story, but they should. James M. Lawson Jr. is an African American Methodist clergyman and a descendent of slaves and escaped slaves, of abolitionists and freedom fighters. Born in 1928 in the American Midwest, he was raised in a family guided by love, soul, and spirit. As a young person, he followed the teachings of Jesus and the Black Social Gospel of uplift for the poor and oppressed. In college, he met A. J. Muste and Bayard Rustin, advocates of nonviolence. They introduced him to the teachings of Mahatma Gandhi, who was assassinated in 1948 after leading a mass movement that overthrew British colonialism in India. Gandhi established nonviolent direct action as a source of power for oppressed people.[2]

Lawson began to engage in what Gandhi called "experiments with truth." As a teenager, Lawson had refused to accede to segregation in public places. In college, instead of accepting his student deferment, he turned in his draft card to protest the Korean War and military conscription and spent thirteen months in federal prison for draft resistance. Upon release, he went to India and learned firsthand about Gandhi's theory and practice of nonviolence. He then traveled through Africa to witness anti-imperialist movements freeing countries from European colonialism.

In February 1957, as a graduate student in theology at Oberlin College, Lawson met the Reverend Dr. Martin Luther King Jr., who had just finished leading a year of boycotts and marches, spending time in jail and suffering death threats and a bombing of his home, to successfully overturn bus segregation in Montgomery, Alabama. King had the experience of using nonviolence in a mass movement, while Lawson deeply understood the history and theory of nonviolence. They instantly recognized their common goal: to replicate the success in Montgomery in using nonviolent struggle to overthrow segregation throughout the South. King urged Lawson to join the Black freedom movement, saying "Don't wait; come now."[3]

From 1957 until King's death in 1968, Lawson and King worked together in a broad framework that went far beyond civil rights to demands for a moral and social revolution. Lawson moved to Nashville, Tennessee, representing the pacifist Fellowship of Reconciliation (FOR), and led workshops on nonviolent philosophy and practice across the South. In cooperation with the Nashville Christian Leadership Conference, a Southern Christian Leadership Conference (SCLC) affiliate, Lawson launched workshops on nonviolent techniques in selected Black Nashville churches. In 1960, intensive role-playing and discussions among Lawson, John Lewis, C. T. Vivian, Diane Nash, Bernard Lafayette, and others in the Nashville student movement helped to launch sit-ins at lunch counters, to spark mass marches, and to fill the jails in an attempt to desegregate downtown Nashville. This cadre joined with freedom riders suffering horrific violence but drawing in federal support to overturn segregation in transportation. They helped form the Student Nonviolent Coordinating Committee (SNCC). Guided by Ella Baker and supported by Lawson, King, and the SCLC, nonviolent organizers continued to challenge white supremacy and segregation in campaign after campaign.[4]

Nonviolence provides a form of moral coercion against one's opposition. But Lawson points out that practicing nonviolence is a harsh discipline, one that requires a willingness to suffer without striking back. Implicit in this is the concept of love in action. King called it agape love, meaning not romantic love or love for family, but love for humankind. In a section called "Pilgrimage to

Rev. James M. Lawson Jr., March 1, 1960. Photograph by Paul Schleicher for the *Nashville Banner*. Nashville Public Library, Special Collections.

Nonviolence" in King's first book, *Stride toward Freedom: The Montgomery Story* (1958), he wrote that nonviolence seeks results without seeking to humiliate or punish one's opponent and directs its coercive power of mass protest and nonviolent resistance "against forces of evil rather than against persons." King and Lawson believed nonviolent action could restore a sense of wholeness to broken communities. "The end is redemption and reconciliation," King wrote. But that can only occur by changing the conditions of life for the better and moving on to new steps toward justice. King and Lawson believed nonviolent struggle could create a "beloved community" that affirms the equal rights and worth of all people.[5]

King and Lawson rejected the characterization of nonviolence as passive. They followed Gandhi's call for organized, active, nonviolent resistance, not only to "physical violence but also internal violence of the spirit," as King wrote.[6] He emphasized that nonviolence is not sinless because it does not always succeed and it requires its adherents to suffer. He called it a lesser evil, compared to doing nothing or contributing to self-reinforcing cycles of violence. King and Lawson recognized that most people would take up the discipline of nonviolence only as a pragmatic tactic to achieve change, while relatively few would adopt it as a spiritual framework and way of life. Their moral grounding in Social Gospel Christianity also included a secular humanist morality that many people could adopt.[7]

Rev. Lawson emphasizes the pragmatic side of nonviolence. African Americans in the South often had to protect their families and themselves by force against attacks by the Ku Klux Klan and racist vigilantes. The right to self-defense, however, is different from using violence in a mass movement in the streets. Lawson and King emphasized that, on principle, people seeking a nonviolent world should follow nonviolent means. Equally important, Lawson said, attempting to use violence to bring about change in the United States would be self-defeating: "Nonviolent discipline is necessary because you cannot beat the enemy with the enemy's theories and practices. You cannot do it. We do not have the power to beat the CIA or the National Guard or the American military." In a dialogue with the radical antiracist, feminist scholar and activist Angela Davis about movement building, Lawson stressed the pragmatic importance of unity of purpose and mass organization: "We have to find ways to create a new power, and the new power is the power of people who get engaged and are willing to work on developing a plan and a strategy . . . that enables us to work as a people to make change."[8]

The mass media described people like Lawson, King, Lewis, and others, as civil rights leaders, but they could be better described as revolutionaries of nonviolence. Lawson says, "A nonviolent person has made a major decision and a major analysis about violence" that requires resistance to and overturning of all forms of violence, systemic and individual. Lawson seeks a "radical overturning of the systems that hurt and cripple people," through an "aggressive engagement to apply a style of life tempered in love."[9] He argues that nonviolence provides our most effective strategy to change society and describes violence as a failure because it does not solve basic problems, and instead inflicts bitterness, brokenness, and more violence.

Both Lawson and King offered sharp critiques of American capitalism, based on its history of genocide against Native peoples, racial slavery of Africans, the oppression of women, racial apartheid, and labor systems that devalue the life and labor of working people. As early as 1958, King wrote that "the inseparable twin of racial injustice was economic injustice"; in 1962, he put it more strongly: "There are three major social evils . . . the evil of war, the evil of economic injustice, and the evil of racial injustice." Scholars often refer to the intersection of these systemic evils as racial capitalism. Lawson has his own term. He draws upon what Black people in Memphis called the "plantation mentality" of whites who treated Black people like servants, and he calls America's economy "plantation capitalism"—with those at the top of the system viewing the world as their plantation, while exploiting workers and the poor. Based on their opposition to violence in all its forms, King and Lawson were economic radicals.[10]

In 1962, Lawson became the minister of Centenary Methodist Episcopal Church in Memphis, while continuing as a volunteer with SCLC to hold nonviolence workshops supporting voting rights and direct-action campaigns in Mississippi and battlegrounds like Birmingham and Selma, Alabama. This period was what King called the first phase of the freedom movement, culminating in the Civil Rights Act of 1964 and the Voting Rights Act of 1965. But these gains merely secured citizenship rights of Black and Brown people and women that should have been theirs to begin with. Dr. King went further, calling for a "radical revolution of values" and a reordering of priorities to defeat what he called the triple evils of systemic racism, economic inequality, and militarism and the Vietnam war. Rev. Lawson too was strongly antiwar and traveled on a diplomatic mission to Vietnam on King's behalf, as they both continued to press forward in what King described as the most radical phase of the freedom movement.[11]

In 1968, King and Lawson joined forces to apply nonviolent direct action to uplift America's working class and poor. King had

Rev. Lawson with striking Memphis sanitation workers, 1968. *Memphis Press-Scimitar*, Special Collections Department, University of Memphis Libraries.

been traveling nonstop, organizing the multiracial Poor People's Campaign. He wanted to take three thousand people to encamp themselves in Washington DC and demand that Congress and the nation shift priorities from spending money for war to investing in housing, healthcare, income, education, and jobs. Lawson asked King to come to Memphis to support a strike by thirteen hundred Black male sanitation workers demanding union rights, a living wage, and safe, decent working conditions. That epochal strike created what Lawson calls a "threshold moment" linking union organizing and the Black freedom movement. On March 18, although exhausted from nonstop travel, King appeared at a mass rally in Memphis, declaring, "All labor has dignity." He called for a general strike to win union rights and dignity for workers and to open up new demands for economic justice.[12]

On March 28, things went awry. The pages of a Memphis newspaper showed a photo of Lawson and King at a press conference that day in Memphis. King looks grim and weary, and there is frustration and dread on their faces. Lawson, chair of the strike support's strategy committee, along with King and others, had led a mass march during which a few people, most likely including police agents, broke windows and looted stores. That break in march discipline gave the Memphis police an excuse to gas and beat people, leading to the hospitalization of scores of marchers, the police shooting death of sixteen-year-old Larry Payne, and occupation of the city by National Guard troops.

The police riot disrupted King's planned Poor People's Campaign and forced him to return to Memphis to lead another march. On April 3, Lawson accompanied King to his room at the Lorraine Motel to plan their next action. Lawson introduced King that night at Mason Temple, where King gave his last, electrifying speech, vowing that "We, as a people, will get to the promised land." He was assassinated the next day, on Good Friday. Lawson called it a "crucifixion event." The workers went on to win their strike, but the victory came at great cost. Despite losses and hardships, Lawson says, the challenge remains: to endure and to take the movement for a better world further than it has ever gone before.[13]

After Dr. King's untimely death, Rev. Lawson continued to apply nonviolence in difficult, pragmatic movements for change. In 1974, he was called to be the minister of Holman United Methodist Church in Los Angeles, where he not only pastored one of the city's largest predominantly Black congregations, but continued to speak, teach, and organize. While unions have declined in most of the

Rev. Lawson (front row, third from left), AFSCME President Jerry Wurf (third from right), May Reuther (second from right), and UAW President Walter Reuther (far right) march in memory of Martin Luther King Jr. in Memphis on April 8, 1968, shortly after his assassination. Walter P. Reuther Library, Archives of Labor and Urban Affairs, Wayne State University.

United States, they have blossomed in Los Angeles. In the history of America's Black freedom movement leaders, Lawson stands out for his continuing efforts to apply nonviolence to labor struggles. Love and solidarity became twin themes in Los Angeles as immigrants, Black and Brown service workers, teachers, undocumented workers, and others organized and won union rights. Rev. Lawson also supported feminism and gay rights and worked to end American military interventions in Central America and the Middle East, domestic violence, police brutality, mass incarceration, environmental devastation, and other forms of violence. After retiring as a pastor at Holman, he has continued to teach the philosophy and practice of nonviolent struggle at colleges and in communities and through the James Lawson Institute and other institutes promoting nonviolence throughout the United States.[14]

Rev. Lawson calls for an international nonviolent movement to overcome the forces of violence. In his eulogy for Congressman John Lewis on July 30, 2020, he challenged the United States to live up to Lewis's dream of a beloved community: "We need the Congress and the President to work unfalteringly on behalf of every boy and every girl so that every baby born on these shores will have access to the tree of life. That's the only way to honor John Robert Lewis. No other way." Lawson spent time in Parchman Prison in Mississippi and once spent Christmas in the Memphis City Jail; he has been maced and shot at, and repeatedly threatened and arrested. As a young man, he didn't expect to live to age forty. Instead, he went on into his nineties in Los Angeles, where he was arrested for civil disobedience more often than anywhere else. As of this writing, he continues on with his Gandhian "experiments in truth," using nonviolence to continually challenge violence in all its forms.[15]

· • ·

The following talks and dialogues by Rev. Lawson link his prophetic gospel of social justice to his pragmatic practice of nonviolent direct action. He interprets nonviolence not as passive but as "an aggressive engagement in seeking to apply a style of life tempered by love."[16] He provides a practical how-to manual on effective ways to organize, find allies, win strategic gains, and, step by step, build a transformative sense of community. He calls today for a massive nonviolent movement to out-organize the forces of systemic racism and violence.

In chapter 1, taken from Kent Wong's interview for this book with Rev. Lawson on August 18, 2020, he highlights the urgency of adopting the revolutionary philosophy, tactics, and strategy of nonviolence in the wake of the struggles against racial oppression and police violence and to expand democracy and voting rights in the epic year of 2020. He calls on us to remember our history of progressive social change movements in order to make real the democratic principles in the Declaration of Independence, the Bill of Rights, and the preamble to the American Constitution—that all of us are created equal and endowed with the "unalienable rights" of "Life, Liberty, and the pursuit of Happiness." How do we secure those rights? That is the question he addresses throughout this book.

In chapter 2, "Understanding Violence and Nonviolence," Lawson defines violence and nonviolence as opposite methods to bring about change but shows how nonviolence is more powerful. He reminds us of our long nonviolent traditions and focuses on how nonviolent organizing in the South from roughly 1954 to 1973 broke the back of legal segregation. The key thing, he says, is to "begin where you are." But to do that, you need a philosophy and a method. He goes on to address that philosophy and method. Chapters 2 through 5 come from an exceptional series of talks I edited that Rev. Lawson gave in 2008 at the University of Washington, Tacoma, supported by the Harry Bridges Center for Labor Studies and the Graduate School of the University of Washington, as well as his talk at a labor history conference, and from personal interviews and interviews for the film *Love and Solidarity: Rev. James Lawson and Nonviolence in the Search for Workers' Rights.*[17]

In chapter 3, "Steps of a Nonviolent Protest or Movement," Lawson insists that holding a demonstration is not enough. A successful movement calls for research and planning, building a philosophical cadre, practicing nonviolent discipline, and establishing a clear set of goals. As he commented in a dialogue with Angela Davis several years ago, "You can't create a revolutionary change without a strategy. There has to be a plan. It has to be both short-term and long-term."[18] Gandhi listed eleven steps of nonviolence organizing, King listed six, but Lawson boils it down more simply to four. He emphasizes the first step, preparation of individuals and communities for nonviolent struggle, including building a framework in which everyone can participate. His discussion of step two, negotiations, is short because every struggle requires its own power analysis and determination of demands. For step three, direct action, he provides examples of a variety of methods to create pressure for change. In step four, follow-up, he tells us how to acknowledge when we have won a victory, however small, how to consolidate our gains, and how to discern and plan the next step for action.

In chapter 4, "Examples of Social Change through Nonviolence," like Dr King, Lawson links racial and economic justice to various freedom struggles that span the globe. He provides powerful examples from South Africa, Poland, Nashville, Memphis, and Los Angeles of how nonviolent movements have succeeded against great odds and often in the face of tremendous violence. He gives us a more extended treatment of the epochal strike of Black sanitation workers in Memphis, one that he says created a threshold moment linking labor organizing to Black and Brown freedom movements.[19] Last but not least, he touches on economic justice organizing for the poor and for Latinx, Black, Asian Pacific Islander, and white workers in Los Angeles, where unions have had success when focused on low-wage hotel workers, housekeepers, and immigrants, as well as teachers, public employees, and healthcare and essential service workers.

Chapter 5, "Where Do We Go from Here?," draws primarily from speeches and dialogues on economic justice that Rev. Lawson gave before audiences at St. John's Baptist Church and at Shiloh Baptist Church in Tacoma, Washington, in 2008, during the Great Recession and continuing Iraqi and Afghanistan wars. It was a time of disintegrating jobs, spiraling homelessness, and widespread hunger and poverty, not that different from 2020's triple pandemic of COVID-19, racism and police violence, and mass unemployment. Lawson calls on us to challenge racial plantation capitalism as a system through nonviolent action and movements for systemic change.[20]

Chapter 6, "You Have to Do the Truth Part First," provides a dialogue that took place on March 6, 2020, between Rev. Lawson and attorney Bryan Stevenson, the leader of Equal Justice Initiative (EJI), in Montgomery, Alabama. Stevenson hosted Rev. Lawson, UCLA Labor Center director Kent Wong, and union activists from Los Angeles in a private gathering and for a tour of Montgomery and Selma. The EJI has fought death penalty and other cases and promotes education as well as action. It has created a chilling remembrance—in its National Memorial for Peace and Justice and its Legacy Museum—of the lynching of African Americans that historically pervaded the South. At the Equal Justice Initiative, the travelers from LA saw auction places that once held slaves for sale and witnessed an exhibit of hundreds of jars of dirt collected from lynching sites in the United States. Their visit and this dialogue took place a day before the commemoration of Bloody Sunday, on March 7, 2020, marking the day police and sheriffs viciously beat people for demanding voting rights in 1965. It was the last time

Congressman John Lewis would lead people across the Edmund Pettus Bridge and the last time he would greet his friend and mentor James Lawson.

On July 30, 2020, the day of John Lewis's funeral, the *New York Times* released his last testament: "When you see something that is not right, you must say something. You must do something. Democracy is not a state. It is an act, and each generation must do its part to help build what we called the Beloved Community, a nation and world society at peace with itself." Lewis called on the younger generation to be the one that "lays down the heavy burdens of hate at last" so that "peace may finally triumph over violence, aggression and war."[21] Rev. Lawson had recruited and trained John Lewis for the nonviolent campaign in Nashville in 1960. How appropriate, then, for Rev. Lawson, in his nineties, to brave COVID-19 restrictions by flying from Los Angeles to Atlanta to give a eulogy at Congressman Lewis's funeral, calling on us to embrace the meaning of democracy and to build a beloved community by using the tried-and-true methods of nonviolent organizing practiced so faithfully by Lewis.

Chapter 7 presents Kent Wong's brief biography of Rev. Lawson, an edited excerpt from *Nonviolence and Social Movements: The Teachings of Rev. James M. Lawson Jr.* (2016), the first book to capture Rev. Lawson's teachings, published by the UCLA Labor Center. Wong has taught a course on nonviolence and social change with Rev. Lawson at the University of California, Los Angeles, for more than two decades.

Rev. Lawson always asks, as King did, Where do we go from here? He tells us that we can't wait for a great leader and that nonviolent direct action requires constant work; it is not something you teach and then you're done. You learn the philosophy and the

Rev. Lawson and Vice President (then US Senator) Kamala Harris, Selma, March 2020. Courtesy of Kent Wong.

group discipline as you experience successes and failures and try organizing in different situations. He often says of the freedom struggles in the South, "We didn't know what we were doing." Rather, they experimented with truth through nonviolence. He calls on us to study and remember the principles of direct action and organizing that came out of those experiences. This book provides some of the history, philosophy, strategy, and tactics of nonviolence that can provide instructive examples and frameworks for radical change, even though our times now and in the future may be very different from the past.

Rev. Lawson pointed out in his eulogy for John Lewis that the goals of nonviolence movements were never limited to civil and voting rights, but sought to make real the truth that all of us are created equal and endowed with inalienable rights to life, liberty, and the pursuit of happiness. Rev. Lawson calls on us to create a massive, nonviolent movement for social change. "Along the way of life," King wrote, "someone must have sense enough and morality enough to cut off the chain of hate."[22]

1 *The Power of Nonviolence in the Fight for Racial Justice*

I have been teaching nonviolence for the past sixty years, since the launch of the Nashville sit-in campaign in 1960. Although I have taught nonviolence over the decades, this is the first publication that captures my teachings on the four steps to a nonviolent campaign.

Nonviolence is a living and breathing science. It has been called the most powerful force on earth, one that has shaped human history and propelled us forward. Since 1789, the United States has not reached a consensus on the meaning and practice of nonviolence. From 1789 until 1954, the Supreme Court never issued a decision that said all the residents of the United States of America are the people of the United States of America. On the contrary, the Supreme Court declared in several cases that Black people had no human rights that any white person needed to consider. The Supreme Court also said that a corporation is a person and therefore is a recipient of the human rights that God the Creator has given all humankind. And until very recently, the Supreme Court did not acknowledge that women are of equal worth and equal importance in our society.

Why is it that we have the United States badly divided by racism, by sexism, by white supremacy, and by violence, but we do not have a consensus that we can make the Declaration of Independence and the Preamble of the Constitution apply to all? America has been shaped by a history of slavery, genocide, and settler colonialism, with capitalists seeing the world as their plantation. Black people in Memphis used to refer to this as the plantation mentality. The governing theories, philosophies, and practices that shape our political, economic, social, and cultural life are based on what I call plantation capitalism.

The situation after the election on November 3, 2020, illustrates the point that we have not yet developed a human consensus that the Declaration of Independence and the Preamble of the Constitution must be interpreted and understood, with their vast humanistic power for the betterment of the human race. We still contend and struggle with each other to see this nation go forward as "We the people of the United States of America."

Multitudes of Americans do not understand that our present freedoms represent the consequences of three essentially nonviolent movements of the twentieth century: the push by women for the right to vote, especially the period between 1910 and 1920; the labor movement and the worker strikes, from the 1930s to the 1960s; and then what the late Congressman John Lewis has called the nonviolent movement of America, which others have termed the Civil Rights Movement, from 1953 to 1973.

In all three of these major movements, you see millions and millions of people struggling to shape a more democratic society. But the opposition to that today still comes from racism, sexism, and the violence of plantation capitalism. The slow climb in the quality of life for millions of people is not a result of plantation capitalism and big business. The power structures have not done this. The power structures have not made the workplace safer. The improvement of workers' lives hasn't come about by the big banks or the Chamber of Commerce or Congress or the president. It has come about because we the people have done the work to organize.

We have recently experienced perhaps the largest, most creative nonviolent movements that have captured the imagination of the human family. The general term for that campaign is Black Lives Matter, and it has resulted in millions of people in the streets in peaceful marches and largely peaceful demonstrations. In the summer of 2020, it brought together people from all sections of the country in an estimated twenty-four hundred locations in all fifty states, in more than seventy-three hundred demonstrations, as well as in protests in other parts of the world.[1]

In this moment, we need to understand nonviolence more than ever. In the early part of the twentieth century, Gandhi proceeded to experiment with nonviolent struggle and also drew from the religion of Jainism. Nonviolence is a philosophy and a methodology he called "satyagraha," putting together the Indian word *satya*, meaning primarily truth, God, soul, spirit, or love, with *graha*, meaning strength, power, or force. We also call it soul force.

We are now witnessing a struggle in which many different groups that have been recipients of the hostility of the nation have demanded that their rights be recognized and that discrimination against them end. But during much of our history, neither the Supreme Court, nor Congress, nor the White House have been forthright allies for the affirmation or the practical application of these human rights for all the people of our country. Some talk about our past as though it is an ideal past, rather than acknowledge the intense struggles that we have gone through and that continue. In doing so, they belittle and they limit the present moment of conversation and struggle.

The Black Lives Matter movement presents another evolutionary period for the awakening of the American people in this, the United States of America. Millions of us now as never before are demanding that our sociopolitical structures become thoroughly equal, thoroughly democratic, thoroughly just, thoroughly manifesting the total human rights of all the people of this country.

The media talk about tension, while they misplace what the tension is about. The tension is not between political parties or between different understandings of the economy. The tension is in fact about the visions and the dreams in the language of our historical documents and the way we seek to implement them today.

We are perhaps the first generation of the people of the United States of America who are contending with the full spectrum of the issues that afflict the human family. No previous generation has struggled with the wide, huge variety of human issues from the ancient and immediate past that have prevented the human race from advancing as far as we could advance.

This is why the introduction of nonviolent struggle with that language is the most important invention out of the twentieth century leading into the twenty-first century, when we know much more about nonviolent history and nonviolent theory. The twentieth century produced many campaigns that helped us to see the possibilities of nonviolence. We have seen that the way of nonviolent struggle can replace violence, war, hostility, and fear and instead, help us to embrace courage and character.

We must not allow this tension in this struggle to cool off. We must do the work that needs to continue. We need to make an urgent effort, an urgent push to understand the history and practice of nonviolence—even as we understand that we are still neophytes in applying this energy that has always been with the human race—

Rev. Lawson receiving the UCLA Medal, 2018. Courtesy of Reed Hutchinson, UCLA.

and to apply it to our own pragmatic concerns. The nonviolent invention from the twentieth century has another major quality that Americans have not yet carefully examined: it comes from our own long history of nonviolence, it comes from Gandhi, and it comes from Martin Luther King Jr.

In contrast to nonviolence, the way of violent conversation, violent structures of inequity and injustice, is the way that will turn our planet into a hothouse and then into an ice-cold Mars. Military violence, domestic violence, the continued lynching of people in the prison systems and by the police—that system of violence is causing our society to sink into greater and greater chaos, turmoil, confusion, animosity, and division. The contemporary world has too much violent rhetoric and violent means and weaponry. Either the nations and the peoples of the world will pick up nonviolent struggle, or the current way in which the world moves will conclude with the massive suicide of the human race and life as we know it on this planet Earth.

Human life as we know it is such a powerful mysterious stream of energy and powers, and I submit that nonviolence is the only way to make progress for the well-being of the human family. It is the only way we the people of the United States can proceed to make equality, liberty, justice, and the beloved community a reality at every crossroads, in every rural and urban area of this country and the world. There are never any guarantees, but it is important to act as if it were possible to radically transform the world.

2   *Understanding Violence and Nonviolence*

Our society has a very long history of violence, which we largely deny again and again. We pretend that we are the most peaceful people in the world, that it's the other people who are violent. It is very difficult then for people to wrap their heads around the idea that there may be far superior ways of getting things done. Most of us have been weaned and nurtured on the mythology that if you want to make any kind of serious change, violence is the way to do it. A lot of us male people think that if we want to have a stable family, we have to be in charge, and we are the boss. And if this means a little roughness—even physical roughness or abuse—we do it. This is a form of violence that is prevalent across the United States and is not talked about, which makes it much more devastating for children and women and even for the men themselves, though they may not understand this.

Violence thrives at the government level as well. Since World War II, which I lived through as a high school student, we have systematically deserted the Constitution and its historic roots. The Constitution says that civilians will be in charge of the military. The people who wrote that lived in a time when the military was extremely strong, when there were draft acts in Europe and Great

Britain, and many men were drafted for the expansionary adventures of Western Europe. The writers of the Constitution wanted to see if they could slow down that history of tyranny and dictatorship, so they made the president of the United States the commander in chief and gave Congress control and oversight of the budget. All that has largely been thrown out the window. It is now the military and the huge private profiteering industry of war that runs the Congress and the White House. That's the reality.

So when we got hit with terrorist attacks on 9/11/2001, and the whole nation was bewildered and hurting, our president said we must do something. And what is that something? It is, "We go to war." So we go to war. That's an illustration of doing the wrong thing, and it only increased the quagmire and further complicated the issues. It resolved nothing. And that's why a nonviolent perspective says that oftentimes doing nothing, that digging in to analyze and investigate, is better than any kind of immediate action. The kinds of military escalations and violence we have all around the world are proving to be the number one enemy of the human race and especially of women and children.

My point is that it is extremely difficult for us to wrap our heads or hearts or wisdom around the notion that there is such a thing as nonviolence—a nonviolent theory, nonviolent techniques, and nonviolent strategy that can make things change so that in the end, there is a better feeling among a much larger number of people. There may be diehards who disagree. For example, in the Montgomery bus boycott of December 5, 1955, to January 17, 1956, a lot of white people in Montgomery and Alabama were outraged that the bus boycott had effectively stymied a piece of segregation and hatred. The other side of the story in Montgomery, Alabama, was that Black people were treated miserably. There were lots of incidents with bus drivers and police that outraged Black people year after year before they finally did the boycott. But there were still white people at the end who just could not stand it. And so you have people like that still in the United States, who have not yet bothered to do some searching to truly join the human race and to find their own role with human affections, human understanding, and human perspectives.

It's extremely difficult for us to wrap our heads around nonviolence. And yet, most people in the world basically are nonviolent, or they want to be nonviolent. Most people do not raise children by hammering them with abuse or violence; most people starting families try to love one another. Most people do not profess to "an eye for an eye" or "a tooth for a tooth." There is a common human wisdom that Gandhi expressed well when he said, "If you practice an eye for an eye and a tooth for a tooth, very soon everyone is blind and everyone is toothless."

Most people are not supporting the wars in their countries. For example, the women and children in Sudan, who are the major victims there, they do not like war, and they do not like the violence. They do not like the abject overthrowing of their lives and the turmoil, hatred, injuries, and deaths, or the starvation, malnutrition, and hunger. Whether it's Liberia or Sierra Leone or in old Yugoslavia in the nineties, most people do not like war in their midst. People do not want to join an armed rebellion, which is why it is so hard to find soldiers who will submit themselves to the training, the discipline, and the hardship or who are willing to obey the leadership in an armed force. Most people have not joined such efforts. So, I don't think the people of the world are violent per se. But I do think that a lot of the national leadership across the earth is consumed by a lust for power, which makes them horrible leaders for their

Rosa Parks with Dr. Martin Luther King Jr. in the background, Montgomery, 1955. National Archives.

nations. I could name many nations, but I will name only one: the United States of America.

Violence Is Abuse of Power

Let me define two things to begin. I will define violence and compare it to nonviolence. To define violence, let me first define power. Part of my quarrel with passivism or "pacifism" I arrived at in 1947 after I was already experimenting with the passage of scripture in 5:38 Matthew, about turning the other check. People called this passivism or pacifism. As I learned about pacifism, people were talking as if pacifism has no power, and I disagree with that. So I did some study on that and concluded that power can be defined as simply the capacity to achieve purpose, as the ability to make things happen. You have to have a certain power to do that.

The difficulty is that we think of power as electric or nuclear power or the power of Rupert Murdoch through the media, and so forth. But we need to bring the idea of power back into our own understanding and under our own control. If you watch the birth and growth of a baby, you will see power. You see the power of physical development—the development of the eyes, the hands, the toes, the limbs. You see the power of curiosity. You see the baby pushing to sit up, to crawl. That's all power, friends. And one of my definitions of nonviolence is that it is the creative energy that we each receive with birth and with life. It can take a variety of forms—mental, social, language, thought—but it is power. Part of our problem is we get confused in our social and political environments to think that we have no power when in fact we were birthed with it. This is not original with me. Aristotle said that power is the capacity to accomplish purpose.

So that said, I will define violence. Violence is the use of power to harass, intimidate, injure, shackle, kill, or destroy a person or persons. It is accomplishing a purpose that is negative, that is intimidation, harassment to persons or a village or a nation, with the result that we deprive the people we're pushing against of their right to shape their own lives and their access to the things that make life possible. So sexism is a form of violence. Racism is a form of violence. Those are structural violence. Slavery was kept in place by violence. Sexism is kept in place through the abuse of and violence against women and children. Violence is an abuse of power. It is a misuse of power. And my contention is that while many people may have the power to do such things, I maintain they have no right to do such things. They are usurping rights. And remember that the Declaration of Independence declares that we hold these truths to be self-evident: that all are created equal, that all are endowed with certain unalienable rights, that among these are life, liberty, and the pursuit of happiness. That is power. And violence is the abuse of power. Violence is not about simply physically beating up, injuring, or killing. It's about intimidation. It's about harassment. It is about seeing other human beings as less than human. Nothing is more dangerous to the United States and to its three-hundred-plus million people than the public conversation, the education, that teaches us that we are an exceptional people and that we're not like other members of the human race or the human family.

Violence destroys rather than builds. Violence prevents human beings from putting the issues on the table and conjuring up the courage to look at them from the perspective of seeking a solution, healing, and the sort of compromises that lead you a little bit in the right direction. Violence destroys and hates. Violence against violence escalates violence. It doesn't solve any of the human problems. Give some of us nonviolent religious people in the United States all the money we are spending on war and the military and the freedom to put it to work for a different society, and in a decade, you will have a different society in this land of ours.

I have named sexism and racism as violence. I can add materialism and greed as other -isms, and these have taught many of us not to respect one another and to be suspicious of our own worth. It is not common sense to believe that I have been created in the likeness of the universe and the likeness of life and the likeness of God, but you haven't, and you haven't, and you haven't, and you haven't. It makes me insecure and suspicious of my own worth if I believe that other people don't exemplify the creative force that I claim for myself.

Violence Is Ineffective

The social theorists tell us that you cannot have a violent revolution if you have a monopoly of military power in the hands of the government. I used to say in the South in the sixties and the fifties, "If you want to use violence, are you going to have sufficient numbers of troops to beat the local police or the sheriff and his forces?" If you are going to prepare for a violent conflict, you are going to have to do it underground, you are going to have to have a high degree of discipline and secrecy, and you better have at least a sufficient force that you can take on the local police and beat them at their own game. And then if you are able to beat the local police, you better be able to beat the state police, then the National Guard, then the Navy, then the Army. There are militia groups talking about a race war in the United States, and they are talking about a war against the government. That is sheer nonsense. They may do fine in their mock wars in the woods of Michigan or Texas, but they could not fight the US government and its military. Even a man like Jesus nearly two thousand years ago told the story of a king who wanted to fight another king for his territory. The first king discovered that the other had ten thousand troops, while he had only five thousand, so he decided wisely that that was not a good venture.

So, there is impracticality to violence. It's ineffective and has been ineffective throughout the world for too many years. We must not let people who romanticize or mythologize violence persuade us that it has proven to be efficacious. It has proven to be the number one enemy of the human race for the last sixty, eighty years, if not before. Since World War II at least, it has proven to be the most ineffective weapon. It drains emotional, psychological, moral, and spiritual energy with no good consequences.

I want to urge you today to the spiritual and moral task of creating a revolution that is utterly necessary in the twenty-first century. And when I use the term revolution, I do not mean violence.

Nonviolence Is a Force More Powerful

From the perspective of Gandhi, nonviolence is the use of power to try to resolve conflicts, injuries, and issues in order to heal and uplift, to solidify community, and to help people take power into their own hands and use their power creatively. Nonviolence makes the effort to use power responsibly. It's personal, and that's why Gandhi spoke of it as a way of life, a lifestyle that determines all of our relationships with one another, the way we deal with our families, friends, and neighbors.

At the root of nonviolence is the notion that within each person there is not only a spark of God, as the Quakers say, but also the spark of love and compassion. I hear many people saying, "I'm not going to love my enemy." As Martin King points out so very well, when Jesus said to love thy enemy, he was not talking about friendship love, nor was he talking about romantic love. He was not talking about deep liking and appreciation. He was talking about what the Quakers and William Penn pledged to the Native Americans during colonial times: how even though we are very different, and we come from different countries and different cultures with many different languages, we have a common human experience that we can show each other and that we can come to respect.

There is no other way. It cannot be done with hatred. It can only be done by people who have compassion and awareness of their own lives in the light of creation. It cannot be done by insulting other people, cannot be done with the gun or the fist, cannot be

1960 Nashville lunch counter sit-in to protest segregation. Nashville Public Library, Special Collections.

done with bombs. We three-hundred-plus million people of the United States can be healed of our fears and our animosities, our hurts and our pains, but that can only happen if we adopt a nonviolent perspective, daring to put the issues on the table in front of us no matter the pain, walking through them and putting together the ethos and principles that can create in the United States a new earth and a new heaven. And I think if religion is valid, as I understand it for myself and for my family, I think religion must get out of the pews and become a movement for the moral, intellectual spirituality that can help us become the people that God has created us to be.

When Jesus said, "Love thy enemy," he meant by that to have respect for the opponent. Do not demonize the opponent. See the opponent as another human being like yourself. That doesn't mean to underestimate the opponent. I have problems with the way professional and university sports are financed, but I nevertheless have great respect for athletics, which I myself have enjoyed all my life and which I have coached. But one of the things I like most about sports is that when you go into a game, you dare not disrespect your opponent. Great football or basketball teams spend a lot of time studying the films of their opponents, studying every member of the other team, because, on any given day, any team can beat the other team. The point I'm making is, that's a good definition of "Love thy enemy."

Don't malign the enemy or demonize the enemy or say all kinds of bad things about the enemy. Know the strengths of the enemy, because your best strategy, in the case of football or politics, is to thoroughly appreciate and understand the enemy as someone who is nevertheless like you—different language, different creed, different culture, different country, but nevertheless fundamentally born out of the creative urge of the universe, out of the creative urge of the Creator. And this is what we have not done in the United States.

In the twenty-first century, we can advance in our self-governance; our ideals can become the tools of our hands and the weapons of our mind and speech. Or we can let things deteriorate to the point that the nonsensical things of violence and war dominate. No matter what happens in the presidential elections, only the people together can make the changes that will forge a new political order and a different perspective of ourselves. I would urge you to that task, to making the economic issue one of the fundamental issues. If a community is afraid to move, then maybe what you have to do is start one on one with people. Don't give speeches like mine or congregational sermons, but instead do quiet study and conversation with one or two people. The nonviolent way is, if you see an issue, you investigate it by pulling together a handful of people and unpacking it until you see some ways that you can work to change it.

That's the first step of the Gandhian methodology called nonviolence.

Soul Force. Spirit Force. Love Force. Truth Force.

I would like to explain some of the influences on India's Mahatma Gandhi. When he was a child, his parents practiced Jainism, a very ancient form of religion in India. It may have been as long as four hundred years before Jesus of Nazareth that they invented a theology or a kind of philosophy called ahimsa, which can be translated, according to Gandhi, as nonviolence. And their principle was that you have to live in such a way that you do not injure life, any life. So in India where Jainism is practiced, you may see a person wearing a mask across his nose and mouth because he does not want to breathe in a gnat and thereby kill the gnat. Gandhi was raised in this philosophy as a child, and he always thought that that was the way that he should live.

In South Africa then, he was trying to figure out what to do about the oppression by the South African government of Indians who had been brought in or immigrated into Africa to build the railroads and to do a lot of the menial work. That sounds familiar here in the United States, doesn't it? But then it turned bad, and they had a lot of nativism and racism going on. As he found himself in the middle of that, he began his experiment in Pretoria. One of the things he did at that time was read the Bible. He was a great reader of all kinds of books, and when he read for the first time the four books on Jesus, he said, "Aha, that's it. That's what I've always believed, and that's what I want to try to do."[1]

In all the wisdom of the human race, there is a cross-fertilization that was an important piece of Gandhi's philosophy. He later said that nonviolence is as ancient as the human race and that it is the best-kept secret of human history. If you read American history books, you do not read about the movements of peace, strikes, or boycotts that effected change on a local level and brought meaningful improvements in people's lives. When Gandhi launched his fifty-year experiment, he did not like any of the terms he'd heard. He did not like "nonresistance," he did not like "passive resistance," he did not like "pacifism," which were all bandied about in certain Christian circles. He liked none of them, so he set out to invent his own word.

He recovered "ahimsa" from his youth and translated it as "nonviolence." But the other thing he did was to have a contest in his newspaper, *Indian Opinion,* out of Pretoria. That was one of the things that he put together for the movement that he was organizing, after some of the first great moments of three thousand or four thousand people tearing up their official governmental ID cards and going to jail to protest the treatment of Indians. He asked, "How do we name this?" He took in suggestions and out of those, he took two words: *satya,* meaning truth, and Gandhi also said that it was synonymous with love, synonymous with spirit; and then *graha,* synonymous with tenacity, synonymous with force, power, firmness, strength. Satyagraha can be translated into the term "soul force," which is the term I most like for nonviolence.

Soul force. Spirit force. Love force. Truth force. Wisdom force. Soul force is a twentieth-century term, and we have to wrap our minds around this. A tremendous number of twentieth-century terms people sometimes want to say came from the eighteenth century or even the first century, and it's not true at all. The terms, for example, homosexuality or heterosexuality—these are twenti-eth-century terms. They were invented toward the end of the nineteenth century, but they were most used in the twentieth century. And I should say that folk who think that these terms are in places like the Bible are quite mistaken. The Bible says no such thing; it hardly mentions anything about human sexuality. So people who want to force into the Bible stuff from the twentieth century are taking on themselves a little bit of tyranny in their interpretations. The point I make here is that satyagraha, soul force, is a twentieth-century term.

One of the great things about Gandhi was that he was not only a speaker but also a writer. Sometimes he wrote as many as three and six hours a day, examining what he was doing and why, putting together his methodology, and collecting nonviolent techniques. It is Gandhi, in fact, who insists that the nonviolent way of doing work is far more rooted in science and reason than violence is, far more rooted in approaching a problem systematically. After fifty years with massive success in South Africa and great success in India, he left us essays and writings that in the Indian government's collection fill one hundred volumes, describing his theory of nonviolence and some of the methodology.[2]

America's Longstanding Traditions of Nonviolence

In our own history, we have had a rather extraordinary story of nonviolent behavior. For example, can you name the colony where there were no killings or wars between the Indigenous people and the settlers for a period of something like seventy-five years? In 1681, William Penn, a Quaker, got a charter from the king to settle the area that we now call Pennsylvania. Before he went to that area, he found the names of Indigenous people and wrote them letters, saying, "We are coming to live with you as neighbors. We are not going to harm you. We respect you. It is our belief"—and it was as radical a belief then as it is now—"that every human being has within them a spark of God, and we want to honor that spark of God in you, as we honor it in ourselves."

For approximately seventy-five years, the Quakers were in charge of the Pennsylvania colony, and not one settler or one Native American was killed. William Penn and John Wohlman went around the colony, talking to the first settlers and to the Native Americans, as a wonderful example of that word that you see in the press often today: evangelicals. They were evangelicals in the best sense of the word. They went about encouraging people to live as sisters and brothers, to live as citizens, common dwellers in the colony of Pennsylvania. There were Indian wars in New York, the north, wars in the east, Delaware, wars in the south, Maryland, and elsewhere. There were no wars in the colony of Pennsylvania for the years that the Quakers had a majority vote and voted in a Quaker policy. That's one of the finest stories in human history anywhere. It is one of the finest stories in our own history, but it's not taught in our schools.[3]

I should say that the word nonviolence was unknown at that time. In 1681, some of the Quakers may have used the term passive resistance; some may have called it nonresistance. Those are two terms in the literature on the history of nonviolence, and they have a fairly ancient past. There is another Christian group called the Anabaptists—the Mennonites and the Brethren—who use the term nonresistance. That word comes from Jesus of Nazareth. Now when I use the name Jesus of Nazareth, I want you to do a little intellectual exercise. Dismiss from your mind, your heart, and your understanding any dogma about Jesus of Nazareth and especially dogma about supernaturalism, supernatural God, and all that stuff. I'm saying this as an active follower of Jesus since a very early age, and I'm saying it as a United Methodist pastor who pastored in churches for forty-three years. The supernaturalism and the dogma of the church about Jesus make it very difficult for the church to really talk about the spirituality or the religion of Jesus. So much of the stuff is *about* Jesus and not *of* Jesus.

Nonresistance comes from the way Jesus himself, in the book of Matthew in the Christian Bible in the fifth chapter beginning at the thirty-eighth verse, says, "Do not violently resist the evildoer," and, "If that person is trying to hurt you, someone knocks you on the one cheek, turn the other. If someone makes you go one mile, go two miles." This is hard stuff, isn't it? But it's a part of the foundation of the theory of nonviolence. And some Christians did call that nonresistance or passive resistance. I am not sure what the Quakers called it, but I think they called it respecting the spark of God in each person and working with that.

So there's a wonderful history of nonviolence in the United States, though that term was not established until the twentieth century, when it was introduced by Mohandas Gandhi of India. I think that each of us has a personal responsibility to try to sense how God speaks to us in terms of the pain that people are experiencing and then to try to organize in the best way we can—and not do it by ourselves but do it with other people—investigate, research, build a little community, and then adopt specific tasks that you are willing to try to accomplish. I think that's the way to go.

Dolores Huerta, Rabbi Steven Jacobs, Rev. Lawson, and Rev. Jesse Jackson celebrate the signing of Los Angeles Hotel Employees and Restaurant Employees International Union Local 11's contract with the University of Southern California, October 5, 1999. Courtesy of James M. Lawson Jr.

Begin Where You Are

In the Nashville movement, I followed that process. We had the Nashville Christian Leadership Conference that would first counsel with a number of excellent human beings to do training on nonviolent struggle, and then we met every week for three to four months. It takes discipline. We assessed our situation in Nashville, and we listed every issue that we could think of that was an unhelpful, unhealthy element in the city for all people, but especially for Black people. And then we went back for another three months, and we examined them with one purpose in mind: in the light of the need for change. For the Montgomery bus boycott, where do we begin? We made the choice by listening to many of the women in those meetings, which would usually include around thirty people. Based on what the women recommended, we said, "We will desegregate downtown Nashville," and that's how the sit-in campaign began in 1959 and 1960.

And when we said desegregate, we did not mean just the ability to buy a hamburger. We meant bringing the "colored" and "white" signs down. We meant jobs for Black people across the community, in banks and stores and so forth. We meant all of those things, and we worked for two or three years there making that happen. So we first did an assessment, and there was a common mind in that assessment of our first task. It was a big task, but we did not try to tackle it as a big task. We took the first piece of it and worked on it, and that helped us to work on many other parts of it in 1960, 1961, and beyond.

So, begin where you are. That's what I say. As anxiety-ridden as that can be, begin where you are in your own situation, and see what happens. But I think the important word is, begin. Let's do it.

3 *Steps of a Nonviolent Protest or Movement*

I want to explain to you the way I teach nonviolent methodology. I took Gandhi as my main source, and in the forties and the fifties I began to hone what I thought were the four major steps.

Step 1: Focus

I call the first step *focus*, and you can add many words to that. Gandhi said the first step was to investigate. I am not sure how useful he found this in South Africa, but I know he practiced it, because all sorts of people, especially people in the villages, came to him to talk to him about their problems. He would insist that they must investigate every facet of the issue that they were bringing to him. Sometimes he went to investigate. Other times, he sent volunteers from his ashrams and his movement to do the investigation.

Investigation means that you become more aware of what the problem is than perhaps anybody else. You educate yourself about it. But as you investigate, educate, and research, you pass on what you're learning to perhaps a handful of people, perhaps a congregation, perhaps a class, perhaps a student body of some kind. But you pass on what you learn so that you help a number of people to begin

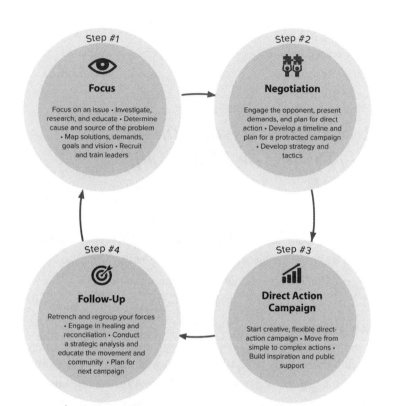

The four steps of a nonviolent protest or movement. Illustration by Lucero Herrera.

to understand the thing that you're discovering or that several of you are investigating.

As you investigate, focus on an issue, give it priority. You then scheme what could be done to resolve it. You begin to map solutions, demands, or ultimatums. Part of your investigation is to find out who is making the decisions that cause that problem to be perpetuated, so you check on that. And in that first step, you begin to recruit people to learn nonviolent struggle, and you help every person to understand the issue to the best of your ability so that you empower them. Everyone ought to be empowered in the nonviolent process. Nonviolence does not have a special elite. In an armed force, you have to use the people who have had the boot camp training, the ability to obey, and a certain amount of physical prowess such that they are able to carry out the actions. But in nonviolence, children, women, men, and young people can be as effective as what one of my friends has called warriors. So you do some basic nonviolence education.

I want to insist on what I say over and over again, that the biggest problem in the United States among the people who see that change needs to take place and are trying to do something is this: they go about it the wrong way. I can name great movements of nonviolence in the twentieth century where decisions were made by certain people that there could be no violence, there had to be nonviolence—like the solidarity movement of Poland where they read the books of King and Gandhi and determined after their failures in the 1970s and 1980 that the next attempt was going to be well planned and strategic and that it was going to be a nonviolent effort.

Part of the problem is you cannot have a nonviolence movement with some people yelling about violence. That will not work, and it causes great confusion and diffusion of strategy. In the movement in the South again and again, when I was the chief organizer in demonstrations, I simply told people who felt they could not stand the heat of the mobs, "Then you don't go this time. You find something else to do." I usually pointed them to some of the work committees, the transportation committees, or the recruiting committees, but said, "You cannot go." I am pretty mean about that. In a movement, you always must have a singular discipline to which all the folk, especially on the action line, commit themselves. The military does not permit people who say, "I'm not in agreement with going to take that hill or that street in Iraq," to be in the military. They take them off the front line immediately. Nonviolence is similar in that way with military strategy.

That first step is a pretty important step and may be the crucial step for making the rest of the effort effective. I use the term *focus* for another reason. All of us involved in the sit-in campaign in Nashville were clergy and students and housewives; all of us were busy folk. Focus has in it a secondary but very important element: priority. I would like to move on fifty different issues, and I'm involved in three of them now. But to start a movement, you have to give up that and go after a single effort together. That's part of what focus is about. When that happens, you accomplish much more than with sporadically running from place to place. I tried to stop being an ambulance or a fire engine chaser as a pastor in Memphis and in Los Angeles. There are always incidents, but I tried to focus in on the issues that I thought I needed to organize around.

So focus. While in that step, you are working on the business of building community for action, getting people informed, and making certain that you have all the information you need for creative action. And you are shaping what you think must happen.

Step 2: Negotiation

You try to go to the powers that be to begin the second step, which is negotiation. The second step does not stop step one; you must intensify step one when you open up the possibility of negotiation. You must let the folk in power you are talking to know that you are

Rev. Lawson leading a nonviolence workshop in Nashville, 1960. Courtesy of National SCLC.

planning a protracted struggle—not one demonstration but many. You must let them know you are working on strategy. Then as you are negotiating, you are also strategizing for the next action step, the agitation in the community to create the soil for the struggle.[1]

Step 3: Direct-Action Movement

For the third step, which is the direct-action movement, you must plan it and work on it. You can start small. In the campaign we can call the Freedom Movement, we had the Montgomery bus boycott in 1955 and 1956, and clustered around that there were economic boycotts in other places. There were all sorts of efforts and strategies and a lot of excitement across the world because the Montgomery bus boycott convinced a lot of people in Africa, Latin America, and Asia that there was hope for change from colonialism to self-determination and the rest of it. There was a lot of excitement in India that the boycott took place and that Martin King emerged as the symbol and the primary strategist and spokesperson for the group.

There were campaigns in 1955 through 1959 that were well established but pretty much unknown. In Nashville, we had a group of people who wanted to take the next step. We used the steps that I am describing for almost eight months of planning, thinking, and choosing the target. That resulted in the Nashville movement that became the pivotal movement for the rest of the sixties, because many of us became the staff people, the volunteers, and the foot soldiers for the 1961 Freedom Ride. Though there were lots of activities, I put the Freedom Rides as the central effort, in 1962 in Albany, Georgia, and in 1963 in Birmingham.

For direct action, it is important to move from simple action to more complex action; it is important to try to escalate the action. While I have been arrested a number of times since the sixties around the country for one-shot campaigns of civil disobedience, I am not a serious advocate for one-shot stuff. I think civil disobedience is one of the big weapons, and movements should escalate to let that happen and to make it happen. By my judgment, you have to have a situation like in Nashville where we overloaded the criminal court system, we overloaded the trials, and we overloaded the police, so that the community was shaken by it all in various ways. Then while direct action is going on, the negotiation should continue, along with the first step of continuing to organize, mobilize, and strengthen the movement.

Then the direct action should reach the pitch of what I call protracted struggle, or disruptive intervention that stops business as usual. It must come to a halt. City councils, city governments, mayors, police, sheriffs, business people, and ordinary citizens must come to recognize we have an issue on hand, and we need to try to resolve it in a fashion that will be helpful to the community. I am a strong advocate for the notion of developing nonviolent action until protracted struggle takes place and business as usual is interrupted and made perplexing. So I am not against disruption of highways and streets, various kinds of boycotts, or lock-ins and sit-ins. Gene Sharp in his historic study of nonviolent weapons published in 1973, *The Politics of Nonviolent Action,* found 198 different techniques for nonviolent action, ranging from the simple button-holing of an official, trying to persuade them of your position or enlisting their effort, all the way to protracted struggle, though he doesn't use that term.[2]

Protracted struggle is a moral struggle that is like warfare, moral warfare. I don't like using that language, but it means that tension is in the air, disruption is in the air, that a lot of people think that their lives have been unduly interrupted. That's a part of the game, and as that goes on, the negotiation goes on. The negotiation, we hope, eventually comes to a good conclusion that the activist group is willing to accept, and you agree to deescalate the effort to consolidate your gains.

Step 4: Follow-Up

The fourth step I call the follow-up. You must first retrench, regroup your forces, evaluate, and see what you have learned, how you can improve it—that is, develop a strategic analysis of the situation.

Secondly, you want to make certain that the agreement that has been reached is going to be carried out. So you need to set up the machinery for the different principles to be followed up on and performed. That's a critical part of it. You must do the healing that needs to be done. If it's a nonviolent action, it will cause a lot of people to change their lives—not all, but some. And you need to corral those feelings and help those feelings to get expressed. This can even be an approach to the people who remain adamant and at enmity with you.

A final part of follow-up is to ask, Is there a next step to what you've just done? Because huge problems in our society are not going to be resolved with one effort. It may take a five-year, ten-year, fifteen-year, or generational effort. The big issue with the politics of assassination in the sixties was that it did not allow that movement to organically develop. And we were developing. We were learning our skills, we were understanding them more, and we were understanding the situation in the United States better.

A lot of people were very naïve and thought that a few demonstrations would change the country. Some of us knew much better than that. Martin King and I talked at length in the year before he died about this, and we were very much in agreement that we had had good success but that we had not dismantled racism, we had not gotten to the structures that uphold it, and we needed to plan the next step for breaking up the institutions and the structures of racism and the like. But the politics of assassination greatly diffused and shocked us and caused many people to drift away, rather than doing what would have been necessary to maintain a dynamic movement.

That is an outline of the nonviolent methodology according to Gandhi. We need people to study Gandhi, King, and the Civil Rights Movement at great length. A lot of the nonsense that I hear

Rev. Lawson and Dr. Martin Luther King Jr., far right and second from right, at a press conference during the 1968 Memphis sanitation workers' strike. Bob Fitch Photography Archive, Department of Special Collections, Stanford University Libraries.

about the Civil Rights Movement is not true. There are some scholars now who are claiming that there was a violent self-defense movement that played a major role. I would like to debate them on that issue. I think that's an erroneous analysis. If you are only interested in your own self-defense, then you don't want to start a movement because a movement is not about self-defense. A movement is about militantly putting yourself at the middle of things and trying to change them, and like any military person who goes into a war or military exercise, you must be prepared to be injured or even killed or severely hurt. You don't go into that thinking that this is a picnic and there are no risks to it.[3]

One of the extraordinary things in the sixties was the great numbers of people who knew the risks—and some people expected to die. I never expected to live beyond forty myself. In Nashville, some people wrote their wills as we proceeded to go on the Freedom Ride. We knew it was that bad; we knew it was that dangerous. And yet there was an extraordinary amount of courage that recognized that suffering and being injured is a part of any significant movement if you want serious change in the right direction. I recommend one other document and that's *A Force More Powerful: A Century of Nonviolent Conflict* by Jack DuVall and Peter Ackerman. How I wish I had had that in 1958. They demonstrate in that book how, in every decade of the twentieth century, literally millions of people used nonviolent strategy, theory, and analysis to create change in their own countries, in their own situations—literally millions and millions of people.[4]

If you are going to have a new society after violence, you have to build it upon egalitarian elements, and you have to help people solve the issues of disease, illiteracy, racism, and sexism and the like. I am persuaded that nonviolence is the only way to manage creative change in the direction of liberty, justice, equality, the beloved community for all—the nonviolence of the spirit, the non-violence of the mind, and the nonviolence of the physical energy, which must always go into a movement.

4 Examples of Social Change through Nonviolence

The South African Struggle for Liberation

I want to urge you today to the spiritual and moral task of creating a revolution that is utterly necessary in the twenty-first century on, and I do not mean through violence. In South Africa, I have met some of the folk who were engaged in the executions of collaborators, young African men mostly, who were part of some of the stuff they carried out in the streets. The danger of the movement in South Africa was the hatred that had poured over into killings. There were several thousand people killed in that period between about 1987 and 1994. It was sporadic killing, some of it by people who disagreed with the African National Congress (ANC) and did not want the ANC to emerge as the primary force in the nation.

Four or five of them who had been street organizers since their teens, when they were in their midtwenties and late twenties, said to themselves, "We're being foolish. This has not worked and is not working and chances are will not work." Some of them went back to what the ANC did in the 1930s to the 1950s and decided to go nonviolent. They called young people and others away from sporadic violence of any kind under martial law, to stop throwing

Bishop Desmond Tutu of South Africa with Dorothy and James Lawson at Holman United Methodist Church, Los Angeles, 1990. Courtesy of Holman United Methodist Church.

stones or Molotov cocktails and the like. Mkhuseli Jack was one of these men I met a couple of times, and he tells that story. You can find that story in the book called *A Force More Powerful*.[1] You can also find it in a book by George Frederickson on nonviolent struggles.[2] Mkhuseli insisted that they begin to organize people in a different fashion and from the perspective of nonviolence.

The common belief is that South Africa had an armed wing, but it never achieved any military objectives. In his autobiography, Nelson Mandela said, "I insisted that it would not be the killing of people; it would be sabotage." He was trying to humanize the violence, and there was some sabotage but it simply did not work. In Port Elizabeth, South Africa, Mkhuseli and others, at the invitation of women in their community, started an economic boycott of the white community. The idea came from women; no one else had thought about it. The ANC hadn't thought about it. And that boycott of white businesses spread like fire across that nation. It brought in people like Desmond Tutu, who was very influential in getting the World Council of Churches to call for divestment and birthed the Free South Africa movement in the United States.

The net result was that the transformation began. Mkhuseli, the first time I heard him talk, said, "We propose with the negotiations that we call for the release of Nelson Mandela," and some of the people from the World Council of Churches said, "Let's not do that. That's political. That won't work." But these young adults said, "No, we're going to include it." It was included and they made their demand. Martial law was declared at least twice, and many of them were thrown in prison and the rest of it, but in the final analysis, the national government began to change and began to have negotiations with Nelson Mandela. In 1990, he was released from prison after twenty-seven years, and this was largely through nonviolence.

Nashville and the Struggle for Freedom

That the Nashville movement was as effective as it became was in large measure because we spent much of nine months assessing the Nashville community and what the issues were that people of color faced, Black people in particular. We met every week, and we went through all the many, many, many issues. We put them on paper and someone took notes. After we made that step, we had a three-month debate on the fact that Montgomery was an important step, that it indicated the efficacy of nonviolent struggle. Now

Rev. Lawson being arrested during the Nashville sit-in movement, 1960. Nashville Public Library, Special Collections.

where can we in Nashville apply this and demonstrate that it can happen again and again? That was our question. And we hashed that out until, in this group of between thirty and fifty people meeting every week, the decision was made that we will begin the process of desegregating downtown Nashville.

The difficulty with some of the reporting on that movement is that it was a sit-in campaign, and I used that term myself because it was the technique we especially lifted up as the beginning place. But it was far more than that, and it continued for almost ten years with campaign after campaign in Nashville. That's an unknown story. But the assessment was to focus on downtown Nashville. No one in the United States was talking about desegregating a downtown area of a city. This is where major segregation took place. There were all kinds of signs, "colored" signs, "white" signs, on drinking fountains, restrooms, all sorts of places where you could not sit down and so forth. It wasn't just the Southeast where this was prevalent. On the West Coast, you had "No Chinese" signs, "No Mexicans" signs, "No Jews" signs, "No Indians" signs. It was really a national disorder of the heart and spirit, and no one talked about that. I don't remember anyone talking about it in the forties or the fifties. I had no idea that desegregating downtown would become the target; it had not occurred to me. But we spent time with people who all had different interests, and some of them were engaged in desegregation of the schools by that time. We came to the common mind that desegregating downtown was exactly the right step to be the next step. And it worked magnificently.

In the beginning of the Birmingham campaign in 1963, in March or late February when we started it, the first demonstration I think we did, we had only fourteen people. But they were ready to go. And oftentimes in those days, we had only fourteen or fifteen at a time, and they were always arrested. But Birmingham moved until we had more than eight thousand people in jail and basically the city immobilized, unable to conduct business as usual. The White House got involved in the negotiations with national businesses that had business in Birmingham, as well as with the governor, the mayor, and businessmen in Birmingham.

And it triggered other demonstrations. In that year, there were more than eight hundred major demonstrations and campaigns across the country. While Birmingham is the central event of 1963 in my judgment, you have to remember that there were many more: 1964, Mississippi Summer; 1965, the voter campaign from Selma to Montgomery; 1966, the Meredith March against Fear; 1966 to '67, the Chicago Campaign; 1968, the Memphis sanitation strike. The year 1968 is when the students at Howard University also launched the movement to improve the curriculum and the university to help them prepare for the twentieth and the twenty-first centuries. So you've got the student movement on campus after campus all through then the rest of the sixties and into the seventies, at Columbia, Stanford, UCLA.

In the Memphis sanitation strike in 1968, six years of organizing persuaded the thirteen hundred men there that they were endowed by the grace of God. This is the way many of them felt and talked, and therefore we walk out, we strike. They didn't ask me or anybody else about it. They knew what was best for them. Some of our folk would say, "You know the unions have a messy background." Yeah, well, churches have a messy background also. But the thirteen hundred men—and they were all men and most of them were Black men—thirteen hundred men came to the point where they said, "We've had enough. We need to change the environment of this work."

These were very poor people, but they were noble people. Some of us who volunteered to raise money wanted to see to it they did not starve, so we got a major relief fund moving, and the union came in and got other unions to come in as we were raising the money. As the unions and we established the pattern of people coming in to some of the offices and churches, we found wives of strikers who kept the cleanest, most detailed ledgers on their little bit of income to make that income stretch as far as they could make it stretch. I said during the strike that if some of these women with these families could become the treasurers of Memphis, of the businesses, and the treasury of the United States, they could really show us how to move the dollar creatively, to feed the children, provide shelter, and all the rest of it.

After that, there were a whole range of actions, with the hospital strikes in 1969 in Memphis, Tennessee, and Columbia, South

Carolina, as examples. You had year after year of major struggles. There was no major source directing this, but it moved mostly as organizations and people organized and wanted to advance the cause of freedom, justice, and equality. So it moved systematically. One must not think of it in any other way than that, because that is the only way that millions of Americans change their minds about the role of government and about racism, segregation, and Jim Crow laws—the only way. In such issues, you can't do this in one effort; it has to be many efforts. And even with that, it did not succeed in dismantling racism, violence, sexism, or economic exploitation that is based on race in the United States, and we have seen the country regress.

Struggles for Racial and Economic Justice: Memphis as a Threshold Moment

When we look back at these movements, we must not pigeonhole them as a civil rights movement per se. In some ways, the bills that got passed in the fifties and the sixties have provided that classification of the movement, and I think that's a massive mistake. It allows a racist country to observe King and the movement in a narrow frame: as primarily a Black thing for Black people. It therefore ignores the huge parameters of the movements of the fifties and sixties, just as we often do with our examination of the labor movement of the thirties, forties, and fifties, and with our examination of the women's movement of the 1910s.

The second remark I want to make is this: on the front lines in the South—in places like Nashville; Birmingham; Jackson, Mississippi; or Montgomery—in the fifties and sixties, our issues were not primarily framed as civil rights. If you go back and look,

Striking Memphis sanitation workers, 1968. Photo copyright Richard L. Copley, used with permission.

for example, at the speech by Martin King on December 5, 1955, you will see that civil rights are not mentioned on the first day of the bus boycott. Justice is mentioned. Liberty and freedom are mentioned. Equality is mentioned. There is also a great review of the nightmare of segregation and racism in this country. Those are the things he summarizes that first day. All through the period, whether in Greenville, Mississippi, or in a more sophisticated situation like Tallahassee, Florida, the slogans were not about civil rights. The slogans were about better jobs. The slogans were about liberty. The slogans were about getting rid of the "white" and "colored" signs in waiting rooms and on drinking fountains all across the South. I think that puts this whole business of what we're talking about, labor and civil rights, in a very different perspective.

The third thing I want to touch on is that a movement of people is never a static affair. A movement is a living organism. It begins in various ways, and it develops in pluralistic ways. But it takes a full generation or two to mature into a conscientious, disciplined struggle that has an analysis that could, perhaps, make a difference in terms of social change. The movement of the fifties and sixties never reached even the age of a toddler. We were all young people, many of us were out of the churches, and we had a sense of high calling. We had a spiritual sense that we were called to do something about it. It was these two passions, nonviolence and spirituality, that linked us and gave us sufficient moxie to take initial steps and to work at it. I like to say that we did not know what we were doing. We only knew that something had to be done about the situation in which we lived.

In Nashville, which was really the ultimate movement for the uniting of mass direct action and for making nonviolence a driving strategy with spirituality, we did not set out to do a sit-in. We set out to desegregate downtown Nashville. This is almost always overlooked. A group of us that, at its largest, included about fifty people and at its smallest, perhaps only twelve or thirteen, spent about nine months strategizing and analyzing the national scene. We assessed our human situation in Nashville. What are the issues that the Black community must live with and deal with day after day? We did this for weeks, and we literally talked about everything that anyone in that group thought ought to be put on the board as an issue. This was a nonviolent process. This was part of the methodology of nonviolence.

After we did that, we asked ourselves the question, Where then should we begin our intervention into all these issues that we see? The group made the decision that we're going to begin by desegregating downtown Nashville. The reason that became the consensus was because of the Black women in those meetings who insisted that "Every day, we must shop in the city of Nashville, with downtown the major place where we can get many of the things we need for our families. And every day we shop is a day of insult. We're open not only to verbal insults but to the indignity of not being able to rest our feet in a seat somewhere, not being able to stop for a cup of coffee in the department store. Where there was a beautiful carousel on the fourth floor, we were not able to stop with our children and let them play while we rested our feet." It was their testimony and their witness, not our superior knowledge, that convinced us that the issue is not the inability to sit in a restaurant and get a sandwich. The issue is the form of apartheid that we live in that no one seems to pay any attention to except the Black people who must accept it or risk their lives, like the Black mothers who must stop their children from drinking at the fountain marked "white," not because they believe in it but because they want their children to be safe. They're protecting their children from the climate in which they live.

Oftentimes in the struggle, we may see what is going on today, but we don't see all the other events and all the other people who have somehow conjoined in a historic moment to make something quite unique happen. That's why the next point I want to make is this: the Memphis sanitation strike was a threshold point for the movement to that date. In a very real way, it was a mark of the growing maturity of the movement. It gave us the chance to join, as we could never have joined in any other fashion, the question of economic exploitation and rapaciousness, the question, as I like to put it, of a capitalism that is fundamentally a plantation capitalism and has not rid itself of that 250-year history. It was the threshold moment and the joining of forces and people and entities that helped us deal with the economic issues.

This issue of jobs was never far away from the movement's life in Memphis. In fact, in the midsixties, we were working on the economic question of jobs. I worked with unions on a minimum wage for working people in the city of Memphis. In Nashville, Tennessee, we said we would not have any negotiating process with the downtown merchants or the city, we would not put the issue of jobs on the table, but we let them know that, while we were calling for the removal of signs and the opening up of public facilities, we would be back the next year with the issue of economic opportunity and jobs. By 1961, we were wrestling with the grocery stores about jobs for Black people, the possibility of people working as supervisors in the stores, and so on. We were always concerned about that question, and Memphis gave us the vehicle to address it. I do not know if I would have thought automatically of a unionizing project as a community social movement and as a justice project for both the union and for the community. I'm not sure I would have conceived of that as a preliminary way of getting at that issue at all.

Some of the academic studies of the Civil Rights Movement are very wrong. When they make the height of the Civil Rights Movement the Voting Rights Bill of 1965 or the Civil Rights Bills of 1963 and 1964, they are absolutely wrong. And they are wrong when they cut King's life and work off at Memphis. In one way, Memphis was the signal of a new and different beginning for the struggle. Whether it was also the signal of a new movement for the AFL-CIO, I do not know. But I have built upon what we did in Memphis and in Los Angeles ever since, both in training Los Angeles Hotel Employees and Restaurant Employees International

Rev. Lawson, Dr. Martin Luther King Jr., Rev. Ralph Abernathy, and others at the Lorraine Motel, Memphis, April 3, 1968, the day before King's assassination. Copyright Barney Sellers-USA Today Network.

Union Local 11 members in nonviolent organizing and civil disobedience and in helping them with some of the problems that we've faced over the years with the police.[3] In Los Angeles, we also started Clergy and Laity United for Economic Justice, through which we bring together clergy—Muslim, Catholic, Protestant, and Jewish—and laity, and congregations to become a support base for organizing workers who are poverty workers and to make the issue a moral issue as well as a union issue.

I will always remember the workers in Memphis, many of them half-illiterate, with perhaps a sixth- or seventh-grade education at most, coming out of the regions of the mid-South where oftentimes they were not allowed to be in school for very long and then did sporadic classroom work at best. In the Cotton Belt, which the mid-South represents, Black children went to school only in between the planting season and the harvest season. This meant their education was brief, and they had precisely what we find now in lots of poor and urban schools: no textbooks, very poor equipment, limited curriculum, and all the rest of it. When we talk about public education, we ignore the fact that not wanting some people to really develop an education is a lifelong part of the history of the United States. What goes on today is but a continuation of those consequences of our nearly four-hundred-year history of oppression of Black people. I was deeply impressed with the consensus that a sizable number of Black clergy arrived at—that the union issue and the issue of equality for Black people are one and the same, and they would not permit anyone in the community to try and knock down that notion or see the union as being peripheral.[4] The workers were able to call an almost unanimous strike of the department's fifteen hundred workers. They empowered themselves when they began to express their issue as a justice issue, when they began to express it as an economic issue, and as a cultural and moral issue. It seems to me that we need to very much keep that in mind.

Today, I think we will not be able to find economic justice or social and political equality for working people and young people unless there is coalescence of the AFL-CIO and community organizing. I have started recently to say to the AFL-CIO that, if you had spent the money that you've given to the Democratic Party over the last twenty years to organize Los Angeles instead, I could tell you right now, in a hundred cities across the United States, George W. Bush and other right-wing candidates would never have had a chance. Somehow, we need to shake up the way we look at labor and labor unions; we need to shake up the way churches and religions look at themselves and recognize that we have a common past of advocating, protecting, and defending our social environment.

We must make this change in every respect, and that must mean, at the heart of it, economic and political justice. It must mean healthcare for every person across our country. It must mean affordable housing. It must mean quality education in every little village in this nation of ours. It must mean stable jobs and jobs that provide the kinds of remunerations that allow people to support themselves and their families, to obtain healthcare, and to shape and influence their own social, economic, and political environment. That's a major lesson that I've learned from Memphis and since. There needs to be a change in the way even academics in labor studies approach civil rights.

Building Nonviolence Internationally

Here is one international example of nonviolence. The Polish saw that their movement in the 1970s was pretty much repressed by the government. At the end of the seventies, a few people got together and said, "We're not giving up. We're going to start over." They studied Gandhi and King, and they insisted, "We're going to be a nonviolent movement. There will be no stone throwing, no Molotov cocktails, no violent rhetoric with one another, no cursing at each other." It's a marvelous story, and they forced the collapse of the dictatorship that was a Communist Party dictatorship. This happened in East Germany, in Czechoslovakia, in Bulgaria, and in a variety of other countries in Eastern Europe. They made a very strong effort to have a thread that bound them together and that worked on their personal lives as well. So, when they did the first big shipyard strike in the early eighties in Gdansk, they locked the gates, and they created a community inside. These workers said there will be no cussing at each other. We will keep the place clean. We will all cooperate in feeding ourselves. We will all take turns cooking and so on. They created a community inside, and that became a pattern all across the nation in factories and shipyards as that movement grew. They recognized that we have to treat one another with dignity, even in the zeal and the often intemperate climate of a crisis.

Building the Labor Movement in Los Angeles

Helping poor workers is a spiritual problem and a spiritual task, because much of the poverty is structured poverty that preys on the souls of the workers. The book of Exodus says at one point that the people could not hear what Moses and Aaron said because of the cruel oppression to which they had been subjected.

Out of a 1996 meeting in Los Angeles came what we called Clergy and Laity United for Economic Justice. We have in that group now Muslims, Jewish rabbis, Roman Catholics, and a variety of Protestant people. I was one of the founders of it, and I was chairman for maybe fifteen years. We have been able to pull together two hundred various congregations whose pastors and congregations, seeing the poverty around them, have for the last several years been looking at the economic situation and asking, "What are their workers doing, and how do they survive?"

Civil disobedience to support Los Angeles airport workers. Left to right, center front, California Labor Federation president Art Pulaski, UNITE HERE Local 11 president Maria Elena Durazo, and LA County Federation of Labor leader Miguel Contreras. Courtesy of Service Employees International Union (SEIU).

We also said to ourselves, "We need to be sure that we as congregational leaders, as local church leaders, are making certain that our support staff people are making decent wages and have healthcare and pension programs," which I have always done anyway as a pastor. So we started with ourselves, started with our congregations. We have had economic justice committees in most of those congregations who are teaching their people about the scriptures and economic justice and about the environment in Los Angeles where they live. And we have ourselves helped poor workers, including helping them organize into unions for the purpose of bargaining for themselves.

Los Angeles is a huge tourist area, a fifteen-billion-dollar tourist area with giant hotels, all sorts of workers, with people coming in from all around the world, and with employers paying people two dollars and three dollars per hour, $4.50 an hour, $6.70 an hour. So we call for living wages. Those workers, many of them all across this country, fear for their jobs. They need their jobs. Most people want to work to earn their own way if they're permitted to. It's a downright lie that some people won't work because they're immoral and lazy. It's a lie that does not bless anybody because the people who tell the lie are cursing themselves; they are saying, "There are so many people who are not like me, and I work and in the sight of God, I'm blessed. But these other folk, they don't and aren't."

So how do you organize a man or a woman who is under harassment and intimidation at their job? You cannot do it there. What I proposed twenty-five or thirty years ago in LA was this: You get the name of a hotel worker or a restaurant worker from a hotel, and you find out where they live. You go to the home and, week after week, you talk to them until the worker is willing to talk about their situation, about their fears, about their family, and about their aspirations. You don't go with the purpose of converting them to anything but for the purpose of letting them connect with another human being who wants to understand their situation and with whom they can build a little bit of community until they find a voice of their own. You know where I learned that from? From the United Methodist Church. It's a form of evangelism, one-on-one evangelism, and it's an effective tool. I used it myself all through my ministry, and I applied it to this working situation. We found it to be a marvelous tool, and we have seen unions use it to build up their ranks.

One of the things that racism, violence, sexism, and greed have taught us is that we are the better people and that there are a lot of people not like us. Racism teaches us that people of color are less than we are, that the Aryan people are superior. That's the

Ku Klux Klan position. Some fifty million people, according to the sociologists of the 1990s, take that KKK theology seriously and live by it. Imagine that, that the Creator made the white people, but all the other people are what they call mud people, created by a demagogue or by Satan. Some fifty million people believe that in the United States today. I'm not trying to demean them in any sense of the word; I am simply saying that racism teaches too many people that their lives have not been created by God and that they are not children of God. And if I believe that about you, it's easy to believe it about myself. That's what Wendell Berry calls the hidden wound, the hole down in the middle of the soul of America.[5]

When people claim that some people in the world only understand violence, that's the same thing. It's a demeaning of their own God-given gift and the God-given gift of the lives of others. Nothing is more important today, in my judgment, than addressing this. The religious people need to get on it, attend to the hidden wound, the poison that millions of people have in their hearts, as men look at women or as Blacks look at whites or whites look at Blacks. I'm not trying to equalize the responsibility at all. But nothing is more important than the poisons in our hearts. And nonviolence calls that poison violence.

5   *Where Do We Go from Here?*

Where do we go from here? For King, this question primarily meant that we must have nonviolent campaigns that are more comprehensive and more directed and disciplined than anything we have done before, that we are only beginning, and that we know that nonviolent power is the only power that can transform injustice into justice and truth. We know that nonviolent power enhances, enriches, and enlarges human beings who practice it, makes them more confident in their gift of life and in their life's journey, and enables them to see and sense their personal power. Even under the harshest of conditions, nonviolence can prevail and can provide direction.

So where do we go from here, chaos or community? That means to me that in the twenty-first century, activists of all stripes must somehow recognize that their activism is connected to the struggle of every man and woman and child anywhere in the world under whatever circumstances, who is engaged in a quest for life rather than death and a quest for living and loving rather than oppression and injustice. We in the USA who are activists must come to see that this is the work for all humanity.

Secondly, we must see that we cannot do the work of humanity if we do not do the work in the places where we live and work. In the United States, we must have effective, disciplined campaigns of nonviolence. And these must become protracted struggles, not one-day protests and not primarily loud marches, but protracted struggles accomplished by studying the tactics we've seen in our own country and what we've seen through Gandhi and what Gene Sharp has collected in his work.[1] We must see the vast array of weapons that we have available through nonviolent methods and tactics, the vast array of weapons that people have used in the twentieth century and before, that we can use in the twenty-first century. The march may be the weakest tactic, not the strongest. It may be the easiest for helping the adrenaline to flow with a lot of people, but it is an adrenaline that is too quickly drained out of us.

The longer and better use of our energy is like the sit-in campaign of Nashville, the Memphis sanitation strike, the Birmingham campaign of 1963, or the Montgomery bus boycott, the first great example in America history. The bus boycott in Montgomery did not begin December 1, 1955. Jo Ann Robinson and Louise West were boycott supporters who led delegations of Black women to the bus company and to the city government calling for a correction of the mistreatment that they felt in the buses on a daily basis.[2] The twenty-first century needs campaigns similar to the Freedom Rides, the Montgomery bus boycott, the 1964 Freedom Summer, the Selma-to-Montgomery march. Those cannot be imitated, but the spirit, the planning, and the development of a program of direct action that might take one week or six weeks or three months or a year of work and preparation—that kind of disciplined effort is what activists in the United States must learn if we are going to understand the meaning of the movement and the meaning of this question, Where do we go from here, chaos or community?

The nonviolent struggle is the only way for us to take a great idea of the twentieth century, a great theme from the ancient peoples of our human race, and apply it to the twenty-first century. We need those campaigns that build upon the nonviolence movement of the 1950s if the United States is going to move away from the chaos in our struggles today, the tensions of our day, into the path of making into reality, "We hold these truths to be self-evident, that all are created equal."

This is both a political posture and a moral posture. It's also a posture for all the people who have some sense that they are religious or spiritual, that they have a responsibility to live in the light of the love that is in their lives, in the light of the gift that is theirs. It's not either/or stuff; it's all of these things. It is a spiritual, moral, political, cultural, social demand on how we can live in these times of tensions where the powers that be at their worst have come to the fore. But we have to know things can get worse before they get better, because now that those powers are on the surface, in places like the White House, depending on who is in control, the Congress, the Supreme Court, and in statehouses across the country, they are going to be absolutely reluctant to yield in any way. So there has to be an understanding on the part of the rest of us that our opposition has to become measured, planned, and filled with the integrity of life itself if we're going to help the United States get back on course.

Where do we go from here? If you have not seen that topic in the book by Martin King that was written in 1968, I invite you to read it.[3] It is a very contemporary statement. In that book, Dr. King tried to summarize the twelve to thirteen years of the active struggle he symbolized and to point the way for the future. Some of the statements in the book are still true today, and they are still inspiring today. The book was not Martin King's idea alone; the title of the book was a theme that we had been discussing in staff meetings, the movement, and the Southern Christian Leadership Conference that seemed to me to be always a question for us. What's next? Where do we go from here? We were constantly working on it. In 1957, 1958, 1959, it was a constant theme in many of the places where crises were occurring: Little Rock; Memphis; Jackson; St. Augustine, Florida; Montgomery; Birmingham; Charlottesville, Virginia; Greensboro, North Carolina; Columbia, South Carolina.

This needs to be a question that you and I consider today, because we don't know. Martin King added the phrase "chaos or community." It was a question that came from the movement, and it was also a challenge to the nation. We were trying to say in that struggle that the people of our land need to ask themselves what kind of people we are and what kind of government we want for ourselves. Do we want an existence between elections that is primarily about the enhancement of the powerful and the rich? Do we want growing chaos? Do we want more violence? Do we want to increase structural poverty? Or do we want to be a people who can see the bonds of human affections appearing, who become more and more connected to each other across every kind of human division, and who lose the shackles of 250 years of slavery and then of Jim Crow law and the exclusion of women and people of color? Do we want chaos or community?

When I was growing up in Massillon, Ohio, where my father was appointed to a Methodist church when I was four, it was a relatively calm, secure, and safe life for me. There were no guns around to speak of. Even though we fought World War II and I lived through that, there was none of this blatant, rabid nationalism that was arrogant about our role in the world. There were some voices of hatred on issues of race and religious bigotry, but they were few in

Rev. Lawson speaking to undocumented students during the first Dream Summer at the University of California, Los Angeles, June 16, 2011. Courtesy of Pocho Sanchez Strawbridge.

number, and at the height of World War II, they were almost quieted by the unity of the people mobilizing to fight that war. We now have literally thousands of hate voices on radio, television, and websites that divide us.

The chaos has been growing. Out of the movement came resistance to change, and the result was the declaration of a war on drugs and a war on crime. Both of those have been abject failures in the United States and caused us to become the leading nation in the world in putting people in jail and entangling people in a parole system and criminal court system that is the worst in the world. Chaos has grown. It leaves any thoughtful person bewildered. Marijuana does not cause the death, rape, disease, hurt, or broken homes that alcohol does, yet in most states, alcohol is legal and marijuana illegal. What kind of nonsense is that? That's chaos. It can only increase chaos. Alcohol is the deadliest drug and you can see the statistics. You hear the reports all the time. It is the number one drug for criminal activity, number one drug for disease, the number one drug for death, and the number one drug in domestic quarrels that end in injury or death. And yet it's legal, and we act as though that's normal, while other drugs that do not have the same toll on life are illegal. This represents a kind of insanity. It's unethical, it's immoral, and it's shameful.

The chaos has grown. We have become a culture of violence. Far more people of the churches are influenced by the poison—spiritual as well as physical—of racism, sexism, violence, greed, materialism, and the lust for power. Far too many people in the Protestant churches are more influenced by these -isms than they are influenced by Jesus of Nazareth. And far more people who are heard in public are more influenced by what in the United Methodist Church we call the forces of spiritual wickedness than by the spirit of unconditional grace, compassion, and love. That's chaos.

The Iraq war was chaos. You can't get apples from a poison ivy plant. It's simply not possible. You get poison ivy from poison ivy. Jesus said it this way: You cannot get figs from a thistle bush. You cannot get a democratic society from the chaos of the Iraq war. You cannot, you cannot, you cannot. It doesn't happen. The universe is not made in that fashion. Life is not organized in that way, however you think it's organized. You cannot have a better nation when we spend nearly eight hundred billion dollars a year on wars past and present, CIA intelligence wars, military intelligence, and the Pentagon, and where that eight hundred billion dollars comes out of our pockets. A high percentage of that eight hundred billion dollars is profit for big business and big investors. You never see a document that indicates the extent to which private profit is a major portion of the so-called defense budget. You don't know the profit level of the GE Corporation or Citicorp or Boeing. All of that is tax dollars that could go for healthcare, quality education, affordable housing, transportation that makes sense, or jobs for everybody. But it is going to the private corporations.

This government, this Congress, this state can only do wrong with our resources when we allow it to, when we give our consent, when it goes on and we say nothing about it. The Declaration of Independence insists that tyranny cannot exist except when the people consent—that when tyranny reaches a level like it did in 1775, the tyranny of King George, then the people must begin to say no and refuse to be governed in that fashion. We don't teach that period of history very well, but there were all sorts of boycotts in that early part of the eighteenth century: boycotts of British-made goods, boycotts of taxes, the Boston Tea Party, refusal to give bread and board to British troops. There were all kinds of town meetings that agitated about equality. The nation was in an uproar. The settlers of the thirteen colonies were in an uproar as they wanted on the one hand to resist tyranny and, on the other, to know which way they were going to go. In our time, I think that we must increase our personal efforts to say no—not just to Iraq and Iran, Afghanistan, and other wars, but also the Republican party, even the Democrats—to say no to their agenda for the nation rather than their addressing our agenda for the nation.

Laying the Seeds for Change

So where do we go from here? I think that the most important soil that you and I must cultivate is to lay the seeds for the movements of the twenty-first century that will reclaim democracy for the

Protest in Atlanta against the fatal police shooting of Philando Castile and other victims of police brutality, 2016. Copyright Sheila Pree Bright, 2021.

United States, that will reclaim justice, reclaim equality, reclaim liberty for all in the United States. I think that we have to lay the seeds by which we can take government out of the hands of the oligarchy and out of the hands of the military and put it back into the hands of truth and the beloved community. That needs to be our goal in the twenty-first century, and I think that it's a goal that we can achieve if all around the country ordinary people get involved in it.

First, that movement must become an inclusive movement. Let me say what I mean by that. As a pastor and theologian for many years, I have felt that human problems are deeply connected to each other, regardless of who you are, where you live, what your income level is, or the rest of it. Here in the United States, we have made various groups of people have to organize on their own and without the consent of the rest of us. The movement of the fifties and sixties is talked about as the Civil Rights Movement, but we rarely talked about civil rights in Memphis, Nashville, Jackson, Mississippi, or in the jails in Mississippi. We talked about the movement, we talked about freedom, and we talked about justice. We talked about dismantling segregation laws. We talked about making it possible that meaningful employment was available to everyone. We talked about ending sexism. We talked about the need for the American people to be united, one people, to see all of ourselves in the same boat and to recognize that any problem in Mississippi is a problem in New York or Nashville, Tennessee, that a hole in the boat sinks the whole boat. Some don't go free if there is a hole in the boat and the boat is sinking. One for all and all for one.

That kind of spirituality is what I mean by inclusive revolution. We must cut across all the different divisions that empire and economics use to keep us divided from one another and keep us talking about red states or blue states or such nonsense. It must be inclusive. Everyone can be blessed and will be blessed.

Second, it's a revolution of convergence. By that I mean that wrong and evil and oppressive systems spread the poison to everybody and poison the whole body politic. I mentioned racism, sexism, violence, materialism, greed, and the lust for power; all of these -isms have a common spiritual dimension. They poison us into thinking either "I am superior" or "I am less than." They cause us to say that some people are not created equal. We men in the poison of sexism make the decision that women are not our equals, are not equally created by God as moral agents in the world. I increasingly see racism, violence, and sexism as so interconnected that I cannot be for the end of violence if I am not for the end of the systems of sexism. I cannot be in favor of the end of sexism in America if I am not in favor of the dismantling of racism.

That is what I mean by the term convergence. We come from the same source of life. The Declaration of Independence says a Creator gave us life and that our identity is rooted in the Creator, not in the government, not in social schemes. That means, sisters and brothers, that whoever you are, you need to help get your mind around the notion that what affects me affects you, that what affects you affects her, what affects her affects him, in every part of the country. Our scheme has to be that we want a society where no child birthed in our society is excluded or does not have access to what, in my own tradition, we used to call the tree of life. That is convergence.

The third thing that this movement must be is a nonviolent movement. It must be a movement of soul force. It must be a movement that comes out of your own depth of soul. Let me say a word about this because I know that I'm talking Greek to some of you. How, in a culture of violence, when we have been weaned on violence, can I suggest that there is another power that is greater than violence? Violence has not brought the changes that you and I would like. Violence has not brought peace in Iraq or Afghanistan. Our nuclear weapons have not ended the small and large quarrels of our nation. Violence has not produced justice anywhere. Violence has not destroyed ideas. As Martin King said, you can bomb a city, but you can't bomb an idea. You can murder a person, but you cannot destroy that person's idea of what kind of world they want. Violence has been a tremendous waste of time. We have not abolished crime in the United States through the billions of dollars that we have put into the criminal justice system and into prisons; instead, we have made building prisons profitable for private businesses that are now on Wall Street for investors to get rich on.

Perhaps the greatest proponent of nonviolent spirituality and action was Jesus of Nazareth, and everyone knows that, Gandhi said, except the Christians. Christianity in the West supported every sort of war, every weapon. One of the beautiful stories in the New Testament in the book of Luke is the fourth chapter where Jesus has just begun to announce what he thinks to be his call for the Kingdom of God. He returns to Nazareth and reads from the book of Isaiah, and as he tries to explain this, the people turn angry with him. They want to know where he got such wisdom. They say, "You came from Nazareth, so how come you know more than we know about the scripture?" They turn so angry that they organize to take him out of the community and throw him over a precipice, to lynch him. That story ends, however, with Jesus walking through the midst of them and going on his way. He continued his work.

Nonviolence Is the Way Forward for the Twenty-first Century

Nonviolence is a new word. It is a twentieth-century word. We won't find it in ancient literature, though you will find the spirit and the practice of nonviolence there. Nonviolence is the best-kept secret of the human race even though it has been found in almost all the written literature that we have from the dawn of writing. Almost all nations have had some forms of nonviolent practice and behavior and people who have lived that way. But nonviolence is a twentieth-century word. It is a science of social change. As Albert Einstein is the father of physics, so Gandhi of India is the father of nonviolence. He did not invent it, but he spent fifty years

Undocumented students stage a sit-in in John McCain's senate office, Tucson, Arizona, May 7, 2010. Courtesy of Anselmo Rascon.

experimenting with it in South Africa effectively and then in India effectively. And he wrote about it. He's who evoked the term nonviolence, or soul force.

What is nonviolence? Nonviolence is trying to use the power that life gives you in ways that solve problems and heal and transform you and change and transform others. Everyone has the gift of creation and the gift of power. Violence is using power in such a fashion as to kill, intimidate, harass, deny, denigrate others, and injure so that you can have control over them. Nonviolence insists that the power each of us has, the power that we often give to our governments, is a power that, used rightly, can turn violence into nonviolence, can turn cruelty into kindness, can turn untruth into truth, can turn war into peace and justice. Nonviolence insists that ends and means are the same thing, that we do not have control over many of the consequences of our behavior, but if our behavior is true, if our behavior is loving, if our behavior in correcting wrong is right, if our behavior uses good means, we sow the seeds for the consequences that will bear the fruits of righteousness, hope, peace, and joy.

I have discovered through the years as a pastor that there are no problems we human beings cannot resolve if we are willing to take the risk to do it. Human life can be healed, but you cannot be healed if you don't admit what the issues are, if you don't put on the table the pain, the turmoil, the ambiguity, and the fears, and try to conjure up the courage to face those issues and to resolve them in some sort of family way or cooperative way. Nonviolence is not about running away but about developing the inward soul, root, mind, and heart whereby you are facing your own life, you're willing to face the lives of others, and you do it with the equanimity of grace and truth.

Nonviolence does not mean you become a coward in the face of wrong. Let me make that clear. I think the cowardly way is for Congress, the military people in the Pentagon, the presidents, and the vice presidents to order our young people to go fight their wars. I think that's cowardliness. For a very long time, I have said that if you're going to decide to go to war, then you become the general, and you lead the charge. You leave our sons and daughters out of it entirely. Nonviolence is not about running away, being passive, or failing to acknowledge that there is an issue or there is a wrong— like we do in the United States when we deny that we are a violent people, when we deny our racism and sexism. That is the way of cowardliness.

Nonviolence is the only way we the people can make government for us, make government for the right, for the true, and for all of us. There is a wonderful story from Poland in the 1970s and 1980s that demonstrates the possibility of taking over government. I could also use the story from South Africa because it is very often misunderstood. Nonviolence has the power to pull us together if we use it rightly. From 1955 until about 1970, there were all sorts of major nonviolence demonstrations, marches, boycotts, sit-ins, and pushes against the churches, voting registration campaigns, the organizing of parallel institutions, across the country, but especially in the Deep South. In that period, King said there developed the coalition of conscience through which tens of millions of Americans told the president and told Congress that we want to change these things, and so through Congress came some of the most progressive legislation that was ever passed.

Some of the books unfortunately talk about only the Voting Rights Bill of 1965 or the Civil Rights Bill of 1964. Those were important laws, but they were not necessarily the most important laws. In those days, Medicare was passed. It was the beginning of a single-payer insurance for all the people of the United States, which is one of the reasons that George Bush tried to undermine it. That was one of the most effective programs the United States government had ever created for the people. Now the pharmaceutical industry has gotten hold of it, and Congress has made available billions of dollars from the Medicare program for the pharmaceutical industry. Head Start came out of the sixties. The first tax dollars out of the Federal Treasury for making higher education for young people more available came in 1961 and '62. Affordable housing became a major part of the congressional budget in those periods.

The point I make is that all that happened because of a ten-year struggle. It wasn't enough. It didn't get us to where we wanted to be, but it started the process of making our society a nobler, more compassionate land. Nonviolence has that kind of possibility.

Call to Movement

In the twenty-first century, every single one of us must become a center of resistance to the directions our country is going, to the chaos. Every one of us must decide again that "I am somebody," "I am a woman," "I am a man," "I am a young person," and "This government doesn't define me; if it doesn't define me as a human being first and foremost, then I will be an implacable resister of the wrong in our society." Each one of us must become a resister. We do not have an effective resistance movement in the United States against racism, sexism, violence, greed, materialism, or lust for power. We do not have an effective resistance movement. We have no political party that is interested in turning the tables in this land. You and I are increasing our numbers by millions who say no in order that we can say yes. We're the foundation of the twenty-first century, moving these 330 million people away from chaos and toward community.

There is more than enough wealth in this nation, more than sufficient taxes in this land for healthcare to be a single-payer program for everyone across the land. We can have a healthcare plan that is as good as what Congress has and as good as what the president has. The issue is not money; the issue is whether or not we the people will become angry enough and passionate enough to say to our political figures locally, statewide, and nationally, "The time is now. You do that which will help the nation become a better nation for everybody."

I invite you not to be so much concerned about the question, "Where we go from here?" but to make certain that your life and your energy are engaged in the task of resisting the venom in our society with a quiet no—and that your life on the other side of the coin is engaged with all your might to be a person of compassion and truth who stands with all humanity, with human affections, and thereby allows your life to become a prayer for a new earth and a new heaven.

Seth Ranquillo and Ilse Escobar participate in a civil disobedience action in support of immigrant rights outside the Los Angeles Metropolitan Detention Center, December 2013. Courtesy of Adrian Gonzalez.

I think it's very clear the way racism and sexism have taught us to despise people. And to not want to organize on all people's behalf is at the heart of the anti-immigration thing. It's not the first time this has become an American issue. It happened in the twentieth century as well as before in a number of places. We have to say that there is no such thing as an illegal human being. There is no such thing in the sight of God as an undocumented human being. The United Nations Universal Declaration of Human Rights says that the right to move across borders for your own benefit or for the benefit of your family is a human right and that it is the responsibility of the governments to make that happen, rather than throwing all sorts of barriers in the way.

There is more activism today in the United States and in most of our cities than we had in 1940 or in the 1950s or even in the early days of the 1960s. We have all kinds of action groups now, young and old, environmental justice, a whole range like I have never seen in my own lifetime. But people are not developing a thesis of social change that is both personally transforming and transforming of society or of the immediate social environment, and that is a part of the power of a nonviolent philosophy and theory. So I am saying that we have to understand what this is about.

The views of young people on how to create change are crucial at a time when our media is saturated with violence. You have been born in a culture and in a society where the media is geared to get you to dehumanize your gift of life and to turn it over to them. And you're not at fault for having inherited that kind of society. We adults are equally at fault. And it's going to take a long, slow, but steadfast commitment to organizing to change it. So maybe in your high schools and in your churches or community groups, you can come together and talk about this and set yourself a course that in one year or two years, five years, ten years, can have effective results in your situation. That's the nonviolent method, to bring people together, assess the situation, and ask ourselves, "What step do we want to take to begin to move it in a different way?" You can do that in a high school. I know of many instances where high school people have been very dramatic in organizing in a nonviolent fashion and have been very effective. So it's a task to take back your lives.

I say to some of my classes that the one-on-one discipline is a personal thing that you can do to make a better world. Don't pick out ten. Just concentrate on one, and see what you learn from it. Again, I want to emphasize that it is not the youth culture that is wrong. The young people inherit the society in which they're born; they are not monsters from Mars. It is the adult society that has failed the children and the young people, not the other way around. And we adults don't know our history.

Much of the movement of the fifties and sixties included, in some instances, children as young as eight and all sorts of young people as well as the elderly. It was cross-generational. The way we do that again is by not living and working in isolation but trying to bring together initially a handful of people who will come to a common mind, and then increase that handful by one-on-one work to create an intergenerational group. Nonviolence calls for the building of your own community family. I have seen this happen, and this is not something abnormal. But so often, our families are unaware of some of our concerns because we don't do enough cultivating, talking, and visiting in the family.

Nonviolence says that you have to develop a community for organizing. Find a common project and go to work on it. Don't look for projects that can be accomplished overnight. None of the good projects can be accomplished overnight. They take some time. The violence in our society has increased steadily, especially across the last thirty years. We are not going to reverse that in one moment. If we can reach a point in history where we have a president who calls for the end of violence and the escalation of violence and a Congress that begins to cut the defense budget, that will be luck maybe, but it can happen. It's going to take serious organizing, effort, and anguish to reverse what's going on today. I wish I could say something different, but I can't.

I have seen a lot of fierce struggle through the years—folks who are doing two and three and four jobs just to stay alive. Most of the jobs that are bragged about on the business pages or by presidents have been poverty-paying jobs without benefits. In Tacoma or Seattle, you see many security people in buildings, and those people are making minimum wages. Most of them do not have benefits of any kind. One of the major organizing issues I was involved in in LA was the organizing of sixty-five thousand mostly African American and Latino security people, young and old, minimum wage, no safety benefits of any kind. We were able to see them organize their own union, get recognized, and start the process of change. There are hundreds of thousands of such workers across the country, and that's the biggest disorder in the United States. Much of the poverty is structured poverty, like slavery was structured poverty.

The chaos will grow unless we look at what happened in the fifties and sixties, and emulate especially the nonviolence. In order to effect change, we must have millions of us agitating and saying no, agitating and making it visible, agitating and saying, "We're no longer satisfied with business as usual." That is precisely what the movement in the 1950s and 1960s did. It wasn't simply protest stuff. The Birmingham campaign is one example in 1963. We immobilized the city of Birmingham. It was a protracted struggle. We went on week after week, day after day. Sometimes there were such crowds in the downtown area that one could hardly move through them. The economic boycott was effective. The demonstrations we were able to carry out put somewhere in the neighborhood of eight thousand people in the jails in Birmingham alone, from all age groups. The city by and large ceased to function because the movement became so powerful. The net result was that President Kennedy himself got into the act and began to demand of big business, "You get involved in Birmingham and solve these issues and settle the Birmingham campaign."

I have put a certain amount of stress upon what each one of us can do, but the one-on-one organizing is what we have to constantly do. If you have some acquaintances who you know are in the wrong about some issues, practice one-on-one work. Just take one name. Don't take ten names. Look around and figure out an acquaintance that you know is in trouble for whatever reason. Then start systematically to go to that acquaintance and to have face-to-face, one-on-one conversation—not for the purpose of converting them but for the purpose of hearing where they are and getting them to talk about their scene, their aspirations, their hopes. In the process of that, you will discover that the two of you begin to connect with each other as human beings. You will find in the process of listening that there are good, important questions that you need to raise with that person that will help that person move deeper into an analysis of their own story and their own scene. As a consequence, you will begin to build a kind of community with that person that will help that person to find a different voice. I have seen this in both church work and union work across the years.

The chaos in the United States will increase unless there is a change of vision, a change of direction, and unless we the people are willing to move in ways, in nonviolent ways, that can effect real change. I maintain that right-wing political leaders and their ilk cannot win. They're on the wrong side of justice. They're on the wrong side of the world. They're on the wrong side of the legitimate human aspirations of billions of people. They will cause a lot of pain; they have caused a lot of pain. They are laying heavy burdens upon the future. But they will not prevail. The way to make certain that happens is by many of us working to create the twenty-first-century movements of justice.

6 You Have to Do the Truth Part First

A Dialogue between Rev. James M. Lawson Jr.
and Bryan Stevenson at the Equal Justice
Initiative in Montgomery, Alabama

JAMES LAWSON: Nonviolence is a major principle in almost all world religions. It's in the ancient scriptures, whether Buddhist, Jewish, or Christian, the notion that you cannot overcome evil with evil; you can only overcome evil with good. That's a central poetic, scriptural, and religious principle, and in many ways Western civilization has ignored it. Western civilization has assumed that you can gain domination, power, control, and management of ideas by and through evil.

The Black experience and slavery were very different from the way we understand it. Frederick Douglass said that on his plantation in Maryland, all the slaves were forced to sing. Wherever they went on the plantation they would be singing, because that was a way for the overseers in the big house to know where they were and what they were doing. That may be the secret to where the Black spiritual and the Black song came from. One of the astonishing things about the Black song is that it's the most creative liturgy of

Rev. Lawson and Bryan Stevenson, March 6, 2020, Montgomery. Courtesy of Kent Wong.

music and poetry that has ever been produced in this nation. One major dissertation by a musicologist listed more than eight thousand pieces of poetry and liturgy from those songs. In that list, which I have read on a number of occasions, you will find no mention of hate. You will find "We are not slaves, we are children of God," "There's a great camp meeting in the Promised Land," "Steal away to Jesus." How many Black folks know "Steal Away" was the "We Shall Overcome" song in the late seventeenth and early eighteenth centuries? They sang it in Georgia, in Virginia, in South Carolina.

My great-great-grandparents were slaves. My great-grandfather escaped as a teenager with his son. So I have two escaped slaves in my background who went on the Underground Railroad up to Ontario, where my dad was born. Then my dad decided at an early age to come back into the United States to live and work.

I maintain that the first level of resistance on the part of many slaves was this formation of an indomitable spirit inside that said, "I know who I am and what I'm about." Some of the museums I have seen have belittled or ignored the Underground Railroad, the escape into Mexico, the escape in Florida, in the mountains of East Tennessee, the escape through the Underground Railroad going north. But that was a major form of resistance under circumstances that you and I can never really understand.

The beginning of the Black religious experience in the United States is not from salvation doctrines of the church, which are nonsense because the scriptures are not about salvation. The Jewish and Christian Bible is not about a salvation system. It's about encounters of eternity with human beings like ourselves, that raise the question, How ought you to live as a human being? What kind of human being should you become? That's what the scripture is about, always testing who we are and what we are.

The Jewish rabbis in the United States understand this better than Christians. The basis of healing and lifting is not through creed and dogma but discovering one's unity with the creative spirit of the universe and recognizing that that is a power beyond imagination. Gandhi said it was the most powerful force in the universe and that if we in the human race ever learned to understand it and live with it, we'd be surprised what kind of world we would create. Nonviolence is that philosophy, theology, and spirituality, but it's also a whole range of history and methodology.

There are more than two hundred methods and tactics in the nonviolent literature today. They are a way of strategizing about what we're facing and how we can start or continue to dismantle violence, to chip away and get rid of it. Your work in the Equal Justice Initiative (EJI) continues to dismantle layers of racism structured in the very way that society has structured institutional violence.

BRYAN STEVENSON: Thank you so much for that. In many ways, you have just affirmed our institutional arc, the need to provide historical context for the nature of our struggle. I thought we could enforce the rights of people on death row in difficult places by using this structure of "rights." We really thought about our work for a long time like the Underground Railroad: we were going into prisons, and we were getting people out. We didn't want to draw too much attention because we were trying to avoid new barriers. And we did that work for twenty-five years.

About twelve years ago, we began to realize that we were living in a new moment. And the insight that we had then was, I don't think we could win *Brown v. Board of Education* today. I don't think our courts would do something that disruptive on behalf of disfavored people. I don't think there's that commitment. We lost this consciousness about what "rights" was about. And that's when we decided we had to leave the courts or at least spend less time in the courts and build a new narrative outside the courts that began to reckon with this history. That's when we started doing the racial justice work in tandem with the legal work of EJI.

We're still in the courts; we're still fighting. When I moved here in the 1980s, there were fifty-nine markers and monuments to the Confederacy in Montgomery. There still are, but you couldn't find the words "slave," "slavery," or "enslavement" anywhere in this city. They were not to be found. This is a state that loves talking about mid-nineteenth-century history. Confederate Memorial Day is a state holiday. Jefferson Davis's birthday is a state holiday. We don't have Martin Luther King Day in January, but we have

Martin Luther King/Robert E. Lee Day. The two largest high schools in Montgomery are Robert E. Lee High and Jefferson Davis High. People in this state love talking about mid-nineteenth-century history, but you couldn't find the words "slave," "slavery" or "enslavement" anywhere.

Our very simple first act of disruption, consciously, was to put up markers that talk about the domestic slave trade, which was dominant in this region. We're in a building where there was a major slave auction block right up the street. The Alabama River down the street is where thousands of enslaved people were trafficked. We are in the building now that is on the site of a former slave warehouse. All of that became a necessary way to give voice to this history. What you'll see in the museum and memorial is an expansion of this idea, which I'm encouraged to hear you affirm.[1] We have to understand this historical context to appreciate the way forward.

My great-grandfather was also enslaved, in Bowling Green, in Caroline County, Virginia. My grandmother Victoria told me that he learned to read as an enslaved person because he believed one day he would be free. That sense of knowing who you are shaped his worldview. This became a part of his identity. She said after emancipation, the formerly enslaved people would come to their house every night, and he would read the newspaper. There was something about the power to read the newspaper that enchanted her. She would sit next to him and listen to him read. Then she said, "I want to read too." Even though she didn't have a formal education, she became very literate.

She gave that to my mother. My grandmother had ten children; my mother's the youngest. And my mother gave that to me, this desire to know, to understand. My people were poor, but my mom went into debt to buy the World Book Encyclopedia so we would have something to read in our house.

LAWSON: As lawyers like you began to work on the death penalty and got corporate law firms to do pro bono work on the appeals, one of the changes that came about early on was that the American Bar Association came out against the death penalty. The American Bar Association had been in favor of the death penalty, but then they switched. So that indicates the power of your work. By going after the death penalty in many, many different places, in different ways, you eventually will build the groundwork whereby the system will be overturned. In many ways, you can't bring about major social change by a direct assault, like going after the signs in Montgomery that said "white" and "colored." But there are many other places where concerted grassroots effort chips away at the system until change becomes the mainstream.

STEVENSON: You have certainly modeled that kind of strategic and tactical activism throughout your life. And we're just so in awe; we're all just so inspired by that. I certainly regard Rev. Lawson as the expert on this.

What we're trying to do in our museum is to create narrative work around our history. We live in a place where people don't have an informed perspective on our history. One of the things we have to do is to change that. We have to talk about the fact that we live in a postgenocide society. What happened to Native people when Europeans came to this continent was a genocide that killed millions through famine, war, and disease, but we didn't call it a genocide. We made up this false narrative of racial difference, and we said that Native people are savages. And nobody questioned that.

That narrative is what gave rise to two and a half centuries of slavery. What we haven't talked about is that people who enslaved folks in this country didn't want to feel un-Christian. So they had to create a myth, a narrative about Black people that made their enslavement legitimate. They said that Black people aren't as good as white people, Black people aren't fully human, they're not this, they're not that. And it was that narrative of racial difference and the ideology of white supremacy that was created to justify something that becomes the great evil of American slavery.

Then we passed the Thirteenth Amendment. It nominally ends involuntary servitude, but it doesn't say anything about this ideology of racial differences. We argue that slavery didn't end in 1865; it evolved. And then we had this long period where Black people were terrorized and traumatized by lynching, and nobody talks about it.

We're still living in a time where these presumptions of dangerousness and guilt get assigned to Black and Brown people. That's how our clients end up committed to jails and prisons. So, for us, it becomes necessary to talk about this history, to erect this memorial to victims of lynching, to have a museum that uses the word "enslavement" in the title, to create a space where you have to begin reckoning with the violence and the abuse.

We're not talking about this history because we want to punish America. Our goal is not retribution and punishment. Our goal is liberation, and the witnesses I have are the enslaved. Enslaved people were brutalized and tortured and maimed. And yet when emancipation came, they didn't want revenge; they just wanted to live in peace. And the power and the spirit to create a consciousness like that is rooted in what Rev. Lawson was saying about knowing who you are.

In our museum, we have a section up on the wall. Enslaved Black people would use their last quarter to place an ad, looking for loved ones that had been taken away from them a decade ago.

What kind of people do that? They are people who have a capacity for love and community and connection that can't be taken. It can't be disrupted even by the violence of slavery. Tapping into that shapes us. Even though there's a lot in the museum that talks about slavery and at the memorial that talks about lynching, we have just opened up a pavilion with big pictures of people like John Lewis, Rosa Parks, Dr. King, E. D. Nixon, and Jo Ann Robinson.[2] The idea behind it is that we are inviting you to reckon with this history.

Truth and justice, truth and reconciliation, truth and restoration—all of these things are sequential. *You have to do the truth part first.* Otherwise, you won't be able to actually talk honestly about what repair requires or what restoration requires. I do think it's strategic. We're not doing this as an aside from our legal work; we see this as part of our legal work. In the next phase, we'll be taking this consciousness-raising around this history and then go back into court and litigate around some of these injuries, looking for ways to use legal doctrine. In every area of the law, if you violate the law, you don't just have to stop violating the law. You have to provide remedies to the people whose rights you have violated. In fact, in many areas of the law, what we talk about is punitive damages. But in the social justice context, we have this consciousness that all you have to do is get people to stop violating your rights, and then everybody's okay. That's not true.

We are still living with the consequences of a century of disenfranchisement. We're still living with the consequences of the GI Bill not being applied fairly to Black veterans. We don't have wealth because of that. We are facilitating an environment where we tell the truth about this history that then leads to a reckoning with what we had failed to do. To remedy these problems is part of what we see ourselves doing.

Black Lives Matter statue at the National Memorial for Peace and Justice, Montgomery. Courtesy of Equal Justice Initiative.

But it's rooted in the same tactical strategic approaches that we learned from the work that Rev. Lawson has been doing, because that's the way you get to this place. In 1965, after the Voting Rights Act was passed, if we could get back to that space, we'd be arguing something a little different. It's not enough for these states to stop banning and blocking Black folks from voting. They now need to remedy these hundred years of disenfranchisement. I would argue that the Black people in the American South shouldn't have to register to vote. The state of Alabama should be registering every Black person when they turn eighteen years old; the state should be required to go to the homes of Black people and get their votes on election day. In so many areas of the law, that would be not only what is accepted but what is required. We're trying to build this consciousness that is rooted in an understanding of who we are but still imagines what we must become in order to be healthy, to be full, to be complete.

LAWSON: This is where nonviolent struggle is critical. Law may state a certain ethical standard, but it cannot be imposed unless somehow the community itself has come to the place to impose this. That's hard work.

In the beginning of the nonviolent movement in Montgomery, Martin King became the spokesperson and the founder of that struggle. When I came south in January of 1958, I joined the struggle with Dr. King, with the development of the Southern Christian Leadership Conference (SCLC), and with the development of SNCC in 1960. Martin King and people like Fred Shuttlesworth, Robert McCullough in South Carolina, and C.K. Steele in Tallahassee, Florida, were all of the mind that nonviolence was the way forward to desegregate the nation. But the big question was, Where would this happen? And who's going to do it?[3]

So that's actually the foundation of Nashville. I came in as a troubleshooter, as secretary for the Fellowship of Reconciliation, and visited many of the hot spots all across the southeastern part of the country. I spent many days with the Little Rock Nine, helping them to endure the almost unbelievable hostility they had to face at Central High School. They had to fight back, they had to resist; otherwise, their lives would be destroyed. They had to learn how to fight back with intelligence and courage and nonviolence.

After Montgomery, the big issue before SCLC was, Could it happen again? That's why, after eight months of traveling full-time in the southeastern part of the country, I decided that I would organize the second major campaign of nonviolence, to demonstrate that Montgomery was not an accident. In Nashville, Martin King had a number of allies and colleagues who had already organized the chapter of SCLC when I got there in January of 1958. I went to that group, though I was not a member, and we decided to do the second campaign, to make Nashville a place to demonstrate that it could be done again. So that's how that happened.

We spent six months assessing the national scene from the point of view of Black people for the purpose of trying to decide, How do we do it? Where do we do it? And that's when the decision was made to desegregate downtown Nashville. That was Black women's decision. The downtown shopping area was an area of grotesque hostility with no Black clerks. The women in our group assessed this and decided to desegregate downtown Nashville.

In Nashville, we strategized with deep, deep preparation for the struggle. We led four months of workshops on nonviolent struggle, including preparation for being hit or trampled upon or going to jail. We did roleplay to help people figure out how you could resist and stay strong. In the process, we were able to prepare a sizable number of people who became staff people for SNCC, CORE, and the NAACP for voter education for the next decade. Not only John Lewis, Diane Nash, Lester McKinney, Cordell Reagon, but a whole wide range of people worked then in Mississippi, Alabama, Tennessee, and elsewhere in the struggle.[4]

So the Nashville campaign was a systematically planned campaign using Gandhi's four steps: focus to get the target, negotiations, direct action, and then the follow-up. The four steps came from Gandhi.

STEVENSON: I think it's worth reflecting on the difference between power and violence. The power of violence is very apparent, very accessible, and very easy to see. People forget that there are other kinds of power, and other kinds of power can sometimes be more powerful than violence. We're actually having to fight with a different kind of power source. That is why nonviolence was so effective. In 1955 and 1956, people in this community learned that Black people were actually in many ways more powerful than white people, even though Black people didn't have police. But they had this capacity to organize themselves in this disciplined way that was so disruptive that, ultimately, they prevailed and were able to slowly bring down this architecture of segregation.

What's interesting for me about that is that the nation's consciousness around civil rights was ultimately shifted by the power brought by women and children during the crusades and those who were part of Bloody Sunday to resist these forces of traditional power through violence. That's the amazing thing that still inspires so many of us. They showed the power to forgive is greater than the power to condemn.

Your life and your work have been so influential. We are persuaded that for us to succeed, we're going to have to demonstrate a power that is greater than violence, a power that can transcend that cycle of violence, because usually violence leads to more violence.

LAWSON: Violence's greatest power is its power to impose suffering structurally and thereby dominate, control, and manage. That's the major power of violence. The prison system is primarily structural violence to control and stop any changes in the systems of racism and racist violence. But violence does not have the power to heal and reconcile and to build a new community. That has to be done from a different source, a different character.

I sometimes define violence as the misuse of power, because power is a given. Power is at the very essence of life. Life is power. Aristotle said that power is a given in the universe; it is the capacity to achieve tasks and purpose. In that sense, violence is a misuse of power, an abuse of power. Nonviolence seeks to recover the use of power so that it enables life and empowers life. But it is a lonely and longer struggle.

Los Angeles has become the second-densest labor center in the country, with over eight hundred thousand members of labor unions, and the political power of labor in Los Angeles is now evident. It's helped to change California. Labor is trying to understand that political power and use it wisely to produce a good number of political figures and elected officials.

I maintain that the United States is not going to change until we get back to the economy, change plantation capitalism, which is what our economy is. Organizing working people in labor unions and helping them to assume and accept the powers they have as a community, as a union that is working toward justice at every level in their own community, can change many different places all across our country. I think that's one of the grassroots things that can be done, and that's one of the very important illustrations. This is why I've spent as much time as I have with labor. During the sanitation workers' strike in Memphis, when I was chair of the strategy committee, I began to realize this. The workers called their job a plantation. That's where I began to recognize what they were saying. I began to use the term *plantation capitalism*, because those guys impressed me with their understanding of what they were being victimized by. The work does require several different arenas, where groups like that can systematically organize where they are.

That's what I was saying earlier about the Equal Justice Initiative. It's so important. This work is the basis of the change that we will get one day in this country, and it is inevitable, in my judgment.

STEVENSON: I totally agree with that. Understanding the structures and then understanding the strategy and the mechanisms for change can help shape the identity of the people and make it a little harder to be an "I" instead of a "we." That's why this articulation of our economic system and the forces that we are creating are very important. The other part of it is understanding who we are in a broader sense, a global sense, a historical sense.

When you do this kind of work, sometimes you have really difficult days. On those days, I would usually go to the river. The Alabama River's right down the street here. I was looking for a place to just be quiet, a place to be peaceful. And I think when you're engaged in struggle, sometimes you just want that space for refuge.

When I was a child, my grandmother would always say to me, "One day, you are going to hear things." When I was in Virginia, she took me to the slave cabin where my great-grandfather was born. She told me that he used to take her there every month and say, "Listen, Victoria, and see if you hear something." And I never understood what she was talking about when she would tell me this. But there was a time when we started doing this work, I began understanding this history. I went down to the river, and I was thinking about my grandmother, and all of a sudden, I started thinking about all of those enslaved people who were trafficked through that river, who were brought to those rail stations, who were put in those shackles and chains and paraded down Congress Street. And then I thought about what it would be like to be surrounded by four thousand people who were there to lynch you, and I thought about the sounds that I heard described when people were doing the Nashville protest, all of that anger and animosity. And it was burdensome to think about those things. But then, all of a sudden, it felt like I could hear something. And it was the sound of the enslaved being trafficked. It was the anguish of people facing torture and lynching. It was the humiliation of people who were dealing with segregation and brutality. When you go into a prison, there's a sound of anguish and suffering when you step into these dorms. I was sitting there hearing these sounds, and then, the sound started to evolve. And they no longer were sounds of anguish and suffering. In a very odd way, they became sounds of encouragement. I felt like I wasn't just fighting for somebody on death row but fighting for the dignity and humanity of all of these people who have come before, who've been trafficked and enslaved and lynched and segregated.

There is something about being lifted up by the whole of human history, by all who found a way to fight oppression and injustice, all who found a way to love despite the hate and brutality. There was something about being lifted up in that kind of community that shifts your capacity, shifts your identity. You don't think of yourself as an "I" anymore; you think of yourself as a "we."

When we opened the memorial, I was terrified. I was preoccupied with rain. I was worried because I didn't want the rain to mess up our big opening with twenty thousand people. At the dedication service, people were praying and singing. We were dedicating the space, and I'm still worried about the rain. Halfway through the dedication, it just started pouring down, and this thing I'd been dreading, I heard, but all of a sudden, I didn't have dread. At that moment, the rain didn't sound like rain; it sounded like the teardrops of thousands of people who had been lynched finally being recognized.

I do think when we understand our place in this larger struggle and this larger experience, we begin to understand that we are a "we," that we're part of something bigger than us. I think that consciousness is necessary because there will be those moments when

The National Memorial for Peace and Justice, in memory of victims of lynching. Courtesy of Equal Justice Initiative.

you get to the point where you think that you can't go on, that I don't think I can do this. And that's where the "we" becomes so important.

I think that's what's so necessary about recognizing and honoring people who have done as much as this precious human being, this beloved soul. It's not just because we want them to feel good, although we do, but we also want others to understand that they have opened doors. They have built some platforms that the rest of us can stand on. You can see some things you couldn't see until that platform was built. I'm hoping that these sites become portals for people, that you can imagine some things that we just hadn't been able to imagine before. If that's our legacy, if we built a higher platform for others to see, we've made some sounds for others to hear, I think it will reinforce this identity. That kind of identity becomes the kind of struggle that Rev. Lawson just said will prevail, because it's rooted in truth. And many of us believe the truth crushed to earth will rise again. It is the essence of what has shaped our worldview. That's the power. I do think sometimes stepping back and reflecting on that becomes necessary. A lot of times, we don't create space to do that. That's why I think it's been so rich, so rewarding, and so affirming to have people come to the sites.

No one has honored us more than this extraordinary human being, James Lawson. I want to thank you for being here, for taking the time to spend with us. I hope that your time here is as powerful as our time with you.

7 A Brief Biography of James M. Lawson Jr.

KENT WONG

James Morris Lawson Jr. was born in 1928 in Uniontown, Pennsylvania, and raised in Massillon, Ohio. His paternal great-grandfather Dangerfield Lawson escaped slavery in the South after hand-to-hand combat led to the death of his owner. Lawson's harrowing journey to freedom led him to Guelph, Canada, to become a farmer and a preacher. His son Henry married into a family of abolitionists. Henry's son, James Lawson's father, Jacob Morris Lawson, rejected farming to get a college degree from McGill University, something highly unusual for anyone at that time. Jacob changed his name to James and became a minister for the AME Zion church. After his first wife died from an illness after having two children, he married Philane Cover, a nurse and seamstress from Jamaica, who would give birth to ten children. This immigrant family moved first to Pennsylvania and then to Ohio. Lawson Sr. became a circuit-riding preacher who carried a gun to protect himself from potential racist attacks in the South.[1]

Coming out of this family of resisters and abolitionists, James Jr. had an instinct to fight back when attacked. He was four years old when he experienced racism and physical violence for the first time. As he was playing in a local park in Massillon, a child addressed him with a racial epithet, and Lawson hit him. When this happened again in the fourth grade, Lawson returned home and reported the incident to his mother. She reaffirmed him as a person in a soliloquy questioning his use of violence that ended with, "There must be a better way." Lawson recalled this moment as "a numinous experience," defined by mystics and theologians as a moment when the world stands still and you hear voices, but most of all you make decisions. Rev. Lawson recounts thinking to himself, "Never again will I use my fists on the playground when I get angry or when someone else gets angry with me. I do not know what the better way is, but I will find it."[2]

As James got older, he developed a deep awareness of the structural violence, segregation, and racism that pervaded both the culture and the laws of the United States. As a junior in high school attending a youth conference in Indianapolis, he conducted his first sit-in, remaining at the counter of Long's Drugstore for over an hour after he was refused service.[3] While he was in high school, Lawson also determined that he would follow his calling and become a pastor, like his father and grandfather and great-grandfather before him.

In 1946, he received his high school diploma, and the following year, began his studies at Baldwin-Wallace College, a Methodist school in Berea, Ohio. There, he met two influential civil rights and nonviolence leaders, A. J. Muste and Bayard Rustin. Muste, the head of the Fellowship of Reconciliation (FOR), an international pacifist organization, presented a series of campus lectures in the fall of 1947. His talk on Gandhi, presenting a method for resisting racism, segregation, and economic injustice while stressing the futility of violence, particularly struck a chord with the young Lawson. Muste's comments and the two men's subsequent conversation over dinner inspired Lawson to read everything he could on Christian pacifism.[4] In 1948, Lawson met Rustin at a statewide Methodist student conference in Ohio. Rustin, who was active in FOR and the Congress for Racial Equality (CORE), had been arrested in 1947 for his participation in the first of the Freedom Rides, called the Journey of Reconciliation.[5]

Two years before the outbreak of the Korean War in 1950, the United States had reinstated military conscription, presenting Lawson with an ethical dilemma. Although he had registered for the draft when he turned eighteen, Lawson believed that the draft was antithetical to his faith and his sense of justice. He concluded that the draft was immoral, especially as the draft boards were often composed of white businessmen, who would often pick African American instead of white men. "I called myself, by the time I was a sophomore or junior in college, a draft resister," Lawson remembers. "I sent my draft cards back." In the fall of 1950, in his senior year in college, he was arrested for resisting the draft, tried, and sentenced to three years in prison.[6] Lawson could have avoided prison by applying for exemption from the draft as a minister or a student, but he believed in the necessity of actively resisting unfair laws and practices.

The government incarcerated Lawson at a federal work camp in Mill Point, West Virginia. The minimum-security facility held primarily conscientious objectors and moonshiners. Although living quarters were segregated, African American and white prisoners could spend time together in the prison library. Lawson studied books provided by church groups and the families of inmates, and he formed a study group with five white draft resisters. Calling themselves a cell group, they gathered in the library four to five times a week for conversation, prayer, and study. But many of the white prisoners were hostile toward the African American inmates, and they were suspicious of draft resisters. As a result, Lawson and the five draft resisters were labeled troublemakers.[7] Eight months later, they were transferred to the federal penitentiary in Ashland, Kentucky, and placed in maximum-security custody. Lawson served thirteen months in prison before being paroled in 1952. Remarkably, Lawson saw his prison experience not as a time of suffering but as a time of learning and community with other imprisoned nonviolence war resisters. His draft resistance began a lifetime of putting his body on the line with others in service of a higher good.

After his release, Lawson made another remarkable journey when he moved to Nagpur, India. Lawson admired Gandhi and his nation's struggle for freedom and said that he "counted Gandhi as one of my intellectual and spiritual mentors."[8] Lawson's experiences, readings, and interviews with independence leaders in India contributed to the development of his philosophy of nonviolence: "I was able to visit ashrams of Gandhi, pick up books that were not available in the US, and I even had a chance to visit with Prime Minister Nehru, the first prime minister of India, who was perhaps the best democrat of the twentieth century."[9] Though Gandhi had been dead for five years, Lawson studied the creative strategies of nonviolence that had overthrown British imperialism, with the intention of applying the lessons at home. In his biography of Lawson, Ernest M. Limbo notes that Lawson's experiences in India led him to "understand the plight of Blacks in America as but one example of the global oppression of nonwhite peoples."[10]

In December 1955, Lawson read about the Montgomery bus boycott in the *Nagpur Times*.[11] He was elated. The principles of nonviolent resistance that he was studying were being used to oppose

Jim Crow customs and laws in Montgomery in a campaign led by a young Black minister named Martin Luther King Jr. Lawson decided that his next step would be to return to the United States, where he could work to desegregate the South through church-based activism and community organizing. Before returning, however, in April of 1956 he took the next remarkable step in his journey, traveling through Africa for six weeks as independence movements burst forth. He returned to the United States well schooled in the international movements for decolonization from Western imperialism as well as in Gandhian teachings.[12]

Lawson then enrolled in Oberlin College's Graduate School of Theology. The director of the campus YMCA, Harvey Cox, was fascinated by Rev. King and had invited him to present a daylong series of lectures in February 1957. Knowing their shared interests, Cox made certain that Lawson was at a private luncheon for King that day. Recognizing Lawson's unusual breadth of knowledge and experience, King asked Lawson to come south to instruct people in Gandhian and nonviolence principles. Both King and Lawson believed the people's movement to end segregation in Montgomery could be replicated elsewhere. King told Lawson that he was the only American activist with such far-reaching knowledge of Gandhian tactics and philosophy.[13]

Encouraged by King to "Come now" to the South, Lawson dropped out of graduate school. Muste offered him a position as FOR's southern secretary beginning in January 1958. Lawson had the option to work in Atlanta where the African American community was highly organized; the National Association for the Advancement of Colored People (NAACP), for example, had office space, a large membership base, a set leadership, and a set way of thinking. Instead, Lawson chose Nashville so that he could attend Vanderbilt Divinity

School, which was known for having the best theology program in the South. In Nashville and across the South, Lawson began to develop the basis for community-based movements through workshops to prepare the next generation for nonviolent direct action. These efforts would soon blossom throughout the South.

On the surface, Tennessee appeared to have less racial animus than other Southern states. Tennessee's two senators had refused to sign the "Southern Manifesto," a document issued by ninety-six senators from eleven states in the South that declared the US Supreme Court's decision in *Brown v. Board of Education,* which ruled public school segregation unconstitutional, an abuse of judicial power. Tennessee's governor, Frank G. Clement, was far more moderate than other Southern politicians, and there were a number of successful African American colleges in Nashville.[14] However, the majority of African American families still lived below the poverty line, and segregation was a way of life in churches, hospitals, restaurants, schools, and theaters.

Although Lawson was based in Nashville, his FOR field assignments required travel throughout the South to share his teachings on nonviolence. One of his first projects was to support the Little Rock Nine, the African American students whom, in the fall of 1957, mobs had prevented from attending Little Rock Central High School in Arkansas, despite a federal order to desegregate the city's public schools. Lawson held nonviolence workshops in Little Rock from January through May 1958. The first workshop was in the living room of Daisy Bates, the president of the Arkansas State Conference of the NAACP. Lawson met with students and supporters two to three days a week. At one point there were more than one hundred attendees, including white students, parents, and some administrators who supported the Little Rock Nine, as well as other African American students who were seeking admission to the high school. Students and their community supporters persisted and succeeded in integrating the school under armed federal protection.

In 1958, Lawson attended his first meeting of the Southern Christian Leadership Conference (SCLC) in Columbia, South Carolina, where he met with King and led his first workshop on nonviolence. SCLC leaders invited him to travel throughout the South to attend meetings, lead workshops, plan campaigns, and counsel emerging community and student leaders. He worked in Raleigh, Greensboro, and Charlottesville, North Carolina; Jackson, Mississippi; Memphis, Tennessee; Louisville, Kentucky; and Birmingham, Alabama. This marked the beginning of his role as a national leader in the desegregation campaigns that became known as the Civil Rights Movement. In Nashville, Lawson and Rev. Glenn Smiley taught a workshop on nonviolence that was sponsored by Rev. Kelly Miller Smith and the Nashville Christian Leadership Council (NCLC), a chapter of the SCLC.[15]

In May, Lawson met Dorothy Wood, the secretary of the National Council of Churches for Christ. They shared a common commitment to the church and to the desegregation movement. When they went to a performance of the Nashville Symphony, they were ushered from their orchestra seats to a section for African Americans in the balcony; they went back downstairs and informally desegregated Symphony Hall that night.[16] The two married the following year. Their union became a rock that supported their years of nonviolence campaigns, his Methodist ministry, and a family of three children.

In September 1958, Lawson enrolled in Vanderbilt Divinity School. He and leaders of the NCLC began holding regular

Congressman John Lewis and Rev. Lawson in Brown Chapel AME Church, Selma, March 2020. Courtesy of Kent Wong.

Saturday meetings with an intergenerational group of community members who were determined to desegregate downtown Nashville. The group included C. T. Vivian, Dolores Wilkenson, Marion Barry, Jim Bevel, Pauline Knight, Bernard Lafayette, John Lewis, and Diane Nash. Momentum increased when the campaign organizers went public and more people joined the workshops. In February 1960, they launched the Nashville sit-in campaign. During the third week of the campaign, the police arrested Lawson and other leaders of the campaign, along with dozens of students, and the resulting controversy led to his expulsion from Vanderbilt University. The dean of the divinity school and eleven members of the school's faculty resigned in support of Lawson, sparking a national debate.[17] The *New York Times* sided with the university, asking "whether or not the university can be identified with a continuing campaign of mass disobedience of law as a means of protest."[18]

On May 10, 1960, the city of Nashville officially desegregated its downtown lunch counters. Lawson, Lewis, Vivian, Nash, Lafayette, and others had spearheaded a sit-in movement joined with boycotts of businesses and mass demonstrations that broke open the segregation system in that city. The Nashville cadre of nonviolence organizers went on to lead freedom rides, boycotts, and other campaigns to create historic civil and voting rights campaigns. Nonviolence theory and practice helped to guide many of the freedom, peace, and social justice movements from 1953 to 1973 and beyond. Dr. King said, and Rev. Lawson has continued to emphasize, that these movements provided a model of how to change a system of violence and oppression without yourself engaging in violence, providing a path to a beloved community in which all people are supported and valued.

During this same period, Lawson collaborated with Ella Baker, King, and other SCLC members to found the Student Nonviolent Coordinating Committee (SNCC). Three cars of Nashville student activists attended the first SNCC conference, held at Shaw University in Raleigh, and the recently expelled Lawson was the keynote speaker.[19] After the Nashville sit-in campaign, Lawson moved to Boston, where he completed his theology degree at Boston University in August 1960. He then returned to Tennessee, taking a position as pastor at Scott Methodist Church in Shelbyville, fifty miles south of Nashville. He also worked as the director of nonviolent education for the SCLC, a volunteer position that King had asked him to fill. This work took him all over the South, where he presented educational programs and supported a series of nonviolent campaigns.

In early 1961, when the Freedom Ride buses were attacked in Alabama, Lawson, Nash, and others from the Nashville sit-in movement lent their support. Lawson even held a workshop on nonviolence inside one of the buses after it was attacked in Montgomery. He was arrested in Jackson, Mississippi, and sent to Parchman State Prison in Mississippi with Lewis, Vivian, Lafayette, and Bevel. Parchman was as bad as its reputation.[20] Lawson also staffed Birmingham's 1963 desegregation campaign in partnership with Fred Shuttlesworth, a minister and cofounder of the SCLC. In the summer of 1964, Lawson participated in the Mississippi Summer campaign to register African American voters in the face of fierce efforts by white elected officials and law enforcement to block African Americans' access to the polls. He and others again ended up in the dreaded Parchman Prison, a hellhole of oppression.

In 1962, Lawson became pastor of the Centenary Methodist Church in Memphis. In that role, he participated in struggles for justice locally, nationally, and internationally.[21] When the United States began escalating its involvement in the Vietnam War, Lawson engaged in debates within the SCLC that focused on whether to oppose the war. King and Lawson publicly spoke out against the United States' role in Vietnam, challenging other clergy and leaders of the SCLC and the community who saw the peace movement as a distraction from the focus on civil rights. In May 1965, Lawson received a call from King, who asked Lawson to join a peace-seeking mission to Vietnam and Southeast Asia in King's place. That summer, Lawson left for a six-week tour of Cambodia, South Vietnam, Hong Kong, and Australia. He met with officials at the US embassy of each country he visited, journalists from *Time,* and Buddhist spiritual leader Thich Nhat Hanh. Lawson reported back to the National Council of Churches in Australia and prepared reports for the SCLC and FOR that condemned US involvement in the war.

In 1968, Lawson assumed an instrumental leadership position in the historic Memphis sanitation workers' strike that linked civil rights to worker rights and economic justice. When two Black sanitation workers were killed on the job due to faulty equipment during a rainstorm, nearly thirteen hundred sanitation workers walked out to protest unsafe conditions and unequal treatment. Workers decried the city's racially discriminatory labor policies, which denied African American workers paid time off during poor weather conditions while providing time off for their white coworkers. On February 23, the police broke up a peaceful march using mace canisters for the first time against civilians at a peaceful protest in the United States.[22] In response, African American community leaders formed a strategy committee to explore forging an alliance between the workers and the community, and Lawson was named chair.[23] He conducted nonviolence workshops for sanitation workers and their community allies. To advance the demand that all humans be treated with dignity, the workers adopted the now-famous slogan "I *Am* a Man."

The committee called for an economic boycott of downtown Memphis, to step up pressure on the business community and elected officials. They invited prominent leaders, including Rustin, King, and NAACP leader Roy Wilkins to lend their support. On the evening of April 3, 1968, King delivered his famous "mountaintop" speech, in which he called for the fair treatment of Memphis's sanitation workers and commended Lawson, the campaign, and the use of nonviolent tactics. King was assassinated the next day at the Lorraine Motel in Memphis. The sanitation workers prevailed, and a settlement was signed on April 16. The city agreed to recognize the union and to improve wages and working conditions.[24]

The Memphis campaign signaled a step forward in forging partnerships between labor and the Civil Rights Movement. In 1969, Lawson continued that effort when he supported a hospital strike for Black workers in Memphis. He also participated in the Black Monday protests to draw attention to employment discrimination and educational inequity in Memphis. Tens of thousands of Memphis citizens participated in the marches and boycotts of schools and businesses. In December, Lawson was one of several African American leaders who were arrested for their involvement, and he spent that Christmas in jail. With King's death in Memphis, the movement did not stop; Lawson and others continued the nonviolent struggle into many areas, leading to substantial changes in political and social life. Racial and economic justice remained a long way off in Memphis, but the tide had turned toward Black political power and a greater role in civic and political life.[25]

Rev. Lawson called the Memphis strike and community movement in 1968 a "threshold moment" during which labor and freedom movements joined together to challenge racism and plantation capitalism and to demand worker rights through unionization. In 2018, fifty years after King's death, more than ten thousand unionists and freedom advocates gathered in Memphis to commemorate King, and more importantly, to rededicate to his goal of creating a nonviolent movement to bring an end to the "triple evils" of racism, war, and poverty. The event also marked a return to the city for Rev. Lawson, who, during a speech at a mass gathering, raised the roof by denouncing the Trump administration and the Republican Party as racist and reactionary. According to historian Michael Honey, who was there, Lawson's call for a rededication to the transformative ideals and direct-action frameworks of nonviolent people's movements for social change was met by a standing ovation.

In 1974, Lawson moved to Los Angeles to begin his twenty-five-year tenure as the pastor of Holman United Methodist Church. In Los Angeles, he helped to launch civil rights, peace, labor, and immigrant rights campaigns. His work with Black, Brown, Asian, and white hotel and service workers helped to build one of the strongest organized labor and immigrant rights movements in the United States today. While union participation declined in most places, it grew stronger in LA thanks to the involvement of immigrant and Latino workers in alliance with Black, Asian, and white workers. Lawson also met and worked with nonviolence organizers from South Africa and elsewhere across the globe and taught workshops on the basic philosophy and methods of nonviolent direct action to UCLA students, undocumented immigrant youth, and immigrants and workers in LA's service economy.

He participated in marches and meetings against the Vietnam War in both Memphis and Los Angeles and continued to oppose American military interventions. He was appointed president of the local SCLC chapter and, in 1977, vice president of SCLC West, and he continued to build interfaith coalitions for peace and justice. He led Peace Sunday, a large antiwar benefit at the Rose Bowl in June 1982, various antinuclear efforts throughout the 1980s, and peace committees that opposed US colonialist policy in El Salvador, Nicaragua, and Guatemala. When the US-backed Contras, funded and trained by the CIA, threatened to overthrow the Sandinista government in El Salvador, Lawson traveled to the country to meet with members of the Sandinista National Liberation Front. In 1982, he spoke before 125,000 people at a rally against nuclear armament in Berlin. At the time, he was "a pastor at a church and considered this all of what a pastor should be engaged in."[26] In Los Angeles, as a part of an interfaith task force on hunger, Lawson helped organize the Adams-Vermont farmers' market to bring fresh food to the South Los Angeles food desert.

In the late 1980s and into the 1990s, Lawson taught the principles and tactics of nonviolence to Los Angeles union organizers in the hotel and custodial industries. María Elena Durazo, then president of Hotel Employees and Restaurant Employees International Union Local 11, contacted Lawson and asked him to educate her staff and members on the philosophy of nonviolence. She invited Lawson and United Farm Workers president César Chávez to speak to workers in the early 1990s and to advise the union on a campaign at the Hyatt Hotel in downtown Los Angeles. In 1996, Lawson helped found Clergy and Laity United for Economic Justice–Los Angeles, an interfaith organization focused on worker justice, which continues to mobilize the faith-based community to actively support immigrant and workers' rights.[27]

Like the workshops in Nashville and Memphis, the nonviolence training in Los Angeles was grounded in a philosophical and moral understanding of the potential of nonviolent struggle to improve the lives of working people. "I got arrested for labor struggles more in Los Angeles than I ever did in the Civil Rights Movement," Lawson noted.[28] This pioneering work led to the transformation of the labor movement in Los Angeles, embracing immigrant worker organizing, forging labor and community alliances, and developing comprehensive campaigns rooted in nonviolence and civil disobedience. Lawson also participated in the 2003 Immigrant Workers' Freedom Ride, when immigrants from Los Angeles and other major US cities traveled by bus to participate in rallies across the country to lobby for a path to citizenship, culminating in a rally in New Jersey's Liberty State Park, across the harbor from the Statue of Liberty. The event mobilized labor and community partnerships for immigrant rights throughout the country.

Every year since 2002, Rev. Lawson has taught the Nonviolence and Social Movements course with the UCLA Labor Center, providing an opportunity for UCLA students and union activists to learn from his teachings on nonviolence and its application to contemporary social movements. Over the years, hotel workers, janitors, home care workers, and undocumented students have been enrolled in the class. Class participants already engaged in ongoing social justice campaigns inevitably developed a deep appreciation for how Rev. Lawson's and Gandhi's teachings have been applied to major US social movements. Many would follow up with Rev. Lawson before and after class to seek his advice on their work.

Many UCLA undocumented student leaders have taken Rev. Lawson's class over the years. In the last fifteen years, UCLA has emerged as a focal point for the undocumented immigrant student movement, as UCLA students and alumni played a national role in the fight for both the California and federal DREAM Acts, and Deferred Action for Childhood Arrivals. When the students learned about the lunch counter sit-in campaign that successfully desegregated restaurants in the South, they were inspired to embrace the philosophy of nonviolence and civil disobedience in the fight for the rights of immigrant youth. At the 2011 launch of the UCLA Labor Center's Dream Summer program, the first national

Front row, US Congresswoman Terri Sewell, US Senator Kamala Harris, Faith and Politics Institute president Joan Mooney, US House Speaker Nancy Pelosi, US Congressman John Lewis, and Rev. Lawson, crossing the Edmund Pettus Bridge, Selma, March 2020. Courtesy of Kent Wong.

fellowship program for undocumented youth, Rev. Lawson addressed the one hundred youth to encourage them to advance their struggle for justice through the use of creative nonviolence.

In 2014, Rev. Lawson, UCLA Labor Center director Kent Wong, and UCLA professor Kelly Lytle Hernandez taught a graduate seminar on nonviolence. Speakers in the seminar included United Farm Worker cofounder Dolores Huerta, civil rights veteran Bernard Lafayette, and labor leader María Elena Durazo. The students worked with the Labor Center to publish *Nonviolence and Social Movements: The Teachings of Rev. James M. Lawson Jr.,* the first book to capture Rev. Lawson's teachings. This breakthrough publication has been used throughout the country to promote the the-

Rev. Lawson, center, receiving the UCLA Medal, 2018, with UCLA Institute for Research on Labor and Employment director Abel Valenzuela, Los Angeles City Councilmember Mark Ridley-Thomas, UCLA Labor Center director Kent Wong, California Senator Maria Elena Durazo, UCLA Chancellor Gene Block, and UCLA Division of Social Sciences Dean Darnell Hunt. Courtesy of Reed-Hutchinson, UCLA.

ory and practice of nonviolence. The present book is the second to capture Rev. Lawson's teachings on nonviolence and the first to feature Rev. Lawson's talks and dialogues in print.

In 2018, Rev. Lawson was presented with the UCLA Medal, UCLA's highest honor, at a ceremony attended by more than five hundred people on the UCLA campus. Lawson continues to have a profound impact on social justice organizations locally and nationally as he supports liberation and justice movements around the country with nonviolence trainings and speeches. Rev. Lawson continues to call for "the greatest nonviolent movement such as the world has ever seen," one that could turn back the tide of violence and global destruction and lead to the beloved community.[29]

Notes

Introduction

1. James M. Lawson Jr., personal interviews with Michael K. Honey, 2000 and 2004, quoted in Michael K. Honey, *Going Down Jericho Road: The Memphis Strike, Martin Luther King's Last Campaign* (New York: W.W. Norton, 2007), 77; James M. Lawson Jr., paraphrased in the film *Love and Solidarity: Rev. James Lawson and Nonviolence in the Search for Workers' Rights* (Bullfrog Films, 2016).

2. James M. Lawson Jr., personal interviews with Michael K. Honey, March 24, 2000, telephone, and May 5, 2000, Santa Barbara, California, quoted in Honey, *Going Down Jericho Road*; see also David Halberstam, *The Children* (New York: Ballantine, 1998), chapters 2 and 5.

3. James M. Lawson Jr., interviews by Michael K. Honey, February 25–27, 2008, Tacoma, Washington, and August 2015, Los Angeles, California; Lawson interviews for *Love and Solidarity*.

4. For a sampling of the vast literature that exists on King, Lawson, Lewis, and others in the Black freedom and nonviolence movements, see "Source Notes" in Michael K. Honey, *To the Promised Land: Martin Luther King and the Fight for Economic Justice* (New York: W.W. Norton, 2018), 199–224.

5. Martin Luther King Jr., *Stride toward Freedom: The Montgomery Story* (New York: Harper and Row, 1958), 82–85.

6. King, *Stride toward Freedom*, 85.

7. King, *Stride toward Freedom*, 81–82.

8. Angela Davis and Rev. James Lawson Jr., "On Occupy: Roundtable Discussion with Angela Davis and Rev. James Lawson," interview transcript, *Race,*

Poverty and the Environment 18, no. 2 (2011), http://reimaginerpe.org/radio /rpe/davis-lawson.

9. Honey, *Going Down Jericho Road*, 92; Lawson interviews for *Love and Solidarity*.

10. King, *Stride toward Freedom*, 72; and Martin Luther King Jr., *All Labor Has Dignity,* edited by Michael K. Honey (Boston: Beacon Press, 2011), chapter 6. For more on King's economic radicalism, see Honey, *To the Promised Land*.

11. Honey, *Going Down Jericho Road,* 91–97; Martin Luther King Jr., *The Trumpet of Conscience* (New York: Harper and Row, 1967), 32; also see Martin Luther King Jr., *The Autobiography of Martin Luther King, Jr.,* edited by Clayborn Carson (New York: Warner Books, 1998).

12. King, *All Labor Has Dignity*, 167–78.

13. King's last speech is reprinted in King, *All Labor Has Dignity,* 182–95; Lawson quoted in Honey, *Going Down Jericho Road,* 450.

14. For details on the James Lawson Institute and its director Mary E. King, see https://jameslawsoninstitute.org. Vanderbilt University, which once expelled Lawson for organizing the Nashville sit-in movement, has established the James Lawson Professorship and programs to highlight his teachings. On July 1, 2021, Dr. Phillis Sheppard became the inaugural faculty director of Vanderbilt's James Lawson Institute for the Research and Study of Nonviolent Movements to promote research, conversation, and knowledge of nonviolence theory and practice. Rev. Lawson's papers are housed at the Heard Library's Special Collections and Archives. See https://divinity.vanderbilt .edu/jameslawsoninstitute.php.

15. Peter Drier, "The Nonviolent Activist Who Mentored John Lewis," *The Progressive,* August 12, 2020, https://progressive.org/dispatches/activist-mentored-john-lewis-dreier-200812/. See also Peter Dreier, "'A Totally Moral Man': The Life of Nonviolent Organizer Rev. James Lawson," *Truthout*, August 15, 2012, https://truthout.org/articles/a-totally-moral-man-the-life-of-nonviolent-organizer-rev-james-lawson/; and Stefanie Ritoper, "Q&A: UCLA's Kent Wong on the Life and Legacy of a Longtime Civil Rights Activist," *UCLA Newsroom*, April 6, 2016, https://newsroom.ucla.edu/stories/q-a:-ucla-s-kent-wong-on-the-life-and-legacy-of-a-longtime-civil-rights-activist.

16. Honey, *Going Down Jericho Road,* 78.

17. Lawson's Tacoma lectures were supported by the University of Washington Walker-Ames scholarship, the Harry Bridges Center for Labor Studies,

and the University of Washington, Tacoma. He spoke at Shiloh Baptist Church on February 25, 2008, on "Where Do We Go from Here?"; at St. John's Baptist Church on February 26, 2008, on "Dialogue on Economic Justice and the Church"; and at the University of Washington, Tacoma, on February 27, 2008, on "Dialogue on Philosophy and Practice of Nonviolence." For this book's text, Michael K. Honey drew on those talks as well as interviews he conducted with Rev. Lawson for the book *Going Down Jericho Road* and for the film *Love and Solidarity.* "The Memphis Strike as a Threshold Moment" is drawn with permission from "Forty Years since the Memphis Sanitation Strike," by James Lawson, in the journal *Labor: Working-Class History of the Americas* (Duke University Press, 2008).

18. Davis and Lawson, "On Occupy: Roundtable Discussion."

19. James Lawson, "Forty Years since King: The Memphis Sanitation Strike," *Labor* 5, no. 1 (2008): 9–13.

20. For this title, Rev. Lawson drew on Martin Luther King Jr., *Where Do We Go from Here: Chaos or Community?* (New York: Bantam Books, 1967). This was a question King and Lawson often posed to think about how to build the next stage of movements for change.

21. John Lewis, "Together, You Can Redeem the South of Our Nation," *New York Times,* July 30, 2020.

22. King, *Stride toward Freedom,* 85.

1. The Power of Nonviolence in the Fight for Racial Justice

1. Erica Chenoweth and Jeremy Pressman, "This Summer's Black Lives Matter Protesters Were Overwhelmingly Peaceful, Our Research Finds," *Washington Post,* October 16, 2020. For Chenoweth's research on nonviolence and international conflict, see Erica Chenoweth and Maria J. Stephan, *Why Civil Resistance Works: The Strategic Logic of Nonviolent Conflict* (New York: Columbia University Press, 2011).

2. Understanding Violence and Nonviolence

1. Gandhi began as an immigrant lawyer in South Africa with no knowledge of the apartheid system, which he experienced as a member of an in-between, "colored" caste, below the white ruling class and misled to believe they were

above the Black masses. It took him time to understand racism in all its dimensions. Activists today are reexamining Gandhi's early racial views, understanding that they changed dramatically to a universal regard for all human beings regardless of caste, color, or religion. See Mary Elizabeth King, "How South Africa Forced Gandhi to Reckon with Racism and Imperialism," *Waging Nonviolence*, October 1, 2019, https://wagingnonviolence.org/2019/10/south-africa-forced-gandhi-reckon-with-racism-imperialism/; and Mary Elizabeth King, "Can We Celebrate Gandhi's Achievements While Also Learning from His Errors?" *Waging Nonviolence*, October 4, 2019, https://wagingnonviolence.org/2019/10/can-we-celebrate-gandhis-achievements-while-also-learning-from-his-errors/. Caste and religious distinctions would later afflict the independence movement in India, and Gandhi's staunch opposition to both led to his assassination by a Hindu nationalist on January 30, 1948.

2. Rev. Lawson based his own experiments with truth on Gandhi's practice. M. K. Gandhi, *An Autobiography: The Story of My Experiments with Truth* (Boston: Beacon Press, 1957, 1993). See also Anthony C. Siracusa, *Nonviolence before King: The Politics of Being and the Black Freedom Struggle* (Chapel Hill: University of North Carolina Press, 2021).

3. This example is not meant to discount the history of land theft and genocide by Europeans against Native peoples but to point out that nonviolence offered other possibilities.

3. Steps of a Nonviolent Protest or Movement

1. The negotiations in Nashville, Memphis, and every other movement in the South proved lengthy, complicated, and frustrating. Lawson's specialty was teaching nonviolence and movement building, so he says relatively little about the process of these negotiations, which were led mostly by local ministers, civil rights leaders, union representatives, and others, rather than Rev. Lawson.

2. Sharp's three-volume *The Politics of Nonviolent Action* and his other books have had significant influence in struggles around the world. Gene Sharp, *The Politics of Nonviolent Action*, vol. 1, *Power and Struggle*, vol. 2, *The Methods of Nonviolent Action*, vol. 3, *The Dynamics of Nonviolent Action* (Boston: Porter Sargent, 1974).

3. Many in the southern freedom movement, even Dr. King, asserted the right to self-defense if someone attacks your home or person. Many Black

Southerners, especially in rural areas, had weapons to defend their homes and families. Military veterans in groups like the Deacons for Defense sometimes effectively protected movement people. Few if any in the movement quarreled with self-defense when used to protect people in their homes or on an individual basis. Lawson here is talking about the futility of incorporating self-defense into the middle of a mass movement based on nonviolence. In *Stride toward Freedom: The Montgomery Story,* King stresses the importance of nonviolence "as the lesser evil" compared to shedding someone else's blood, but acknowledges that accepting violence against one's self or others is not free from moral dilemmas. Martin Luther King Jr., *Stride toward Freedom: The Montgomery Story* (New York: Harper and Row, 1958), 81. Malcolm X disputed King's emphasis on nonviolence, as did some movement activists in the South and in the Black Panther Party for Self-Defense. Movement veteran Charles E. Cobb posed questions about the role of self-defense in Charles E. Cobb, *This Nonviolent Stuff'll Get You Killed: How Guns Made the Civil Rights Movement Possible* (Durham, NC: Duke University Press, 2015). There are numerous studies of self-defense in the southern movement, including Lance E. Hill, *The Deacons for Defense: Armed Resistance and the Civil Rights Movement* (Chapel Hill: University of North Carolina Press, 2004), and Timothy B. Tyson, *Radio Free Dixie: Robert F. Williams and the Roots of Black Power* (Chapel Hill: University of North Carolina Press, 2001); see also Joshua Bloom and Waldo E. Martin, *Black against Empire: The History and Politics of the Black Panther Party* (Berkeley: University of California Press, 2016).

4. Peter Ackerman and Jack DuVall, *A Force More Powerful: A Century of Nonviolent Conflict* (New York: St. Martin's Press, 2000). For continuing implementation and research on the vision of nonviolent social change, see the International Center on Nonviolent Conflict, https://www.nonviolent-conflict.org/.

4. Examples of Social Change through Nonviolence

1. Peter Ackerman and Jack DuVall, *A Force More Powerful: A Century of Nonviolent Conflict* (New York: St. Martin's Press, 2000).

2. For an early overview, see George M. Frederickson, "Resistance to White Supremacy: Nonviolence in the US South and South Africa," *Dissent* (Winter 1995): 61–70; and George M. Frederickson, *Racism: A Short History* (Princeton, NJ: Princeton University Press, 2002).

3. In 2004, the Hotel Employees and Restaurant Employees International Union merged with the Union of Needletrades, Industrial, and Textile Employees to form UNITE HERE.

4. The local union referred to here is the American Federation of State, County, and Municipal Employees (AFSCME) Local 1733.

5. Wendell Berry, *The Hidden Wound* (Boston: Houghton Mifflin, 1970).

5. Where Do We Go from Here?

1. Gene Sharp, *The Politics of Nonviolent Action*, vol. 1, *Power and Struggle*, vol. 2, *The Methods of Nonviolent Action,* vol. 3, *The Dynamics of Nonviolent Action* (Boston: Porter Sargent, 1974).

2. Women had been fighting transportation racism in Montgomery for a long time. On March 2, 1955, Claudette Colvin was arrested for refusing to go along with bus segregation, and on December 1, 1955, so was Rosa Parks. Parks had long been active in the Civil Rights Movement, and her case set off the year-long bus boycott that brought Martin Luther King Jr. into leadership and electrified James Lawson, who was in India when he read the story. See the account by Jeanne Theoharis, *The Rebellious Life of Mrs. Rosa Parks* (Boston: Beacon Press, 2013).

3. Martin Luther King Jr., *Where Do We Go from Here: Chaos or Community?* (New York: Bantam Books, 1967).

6. You Have to Do the Truth Part First

1. The museum and memorial referred to here are the Legacy Museum and the National Memorial for Peace and Justice, which were created by EJI; see https://museumandmemorial.eji.org/.

2. Rosa Parks, a long-time Black civil rights activist in Montgomery who refused to give up her seat on a bus on December 1, 1955, was arrested and inspired a bus boycott that lasted over a year. She worked closely with Edgar Daniel Nixon, the local NAACP president and a leader in the Pullman Porters Union, and both played a key role in the boycott. Jo Ann Robinson worked at a local college and led the Women's Political Council, a group of Black women activists who turned out thousands of leaflets to start the boycott. King served as spokesman, but others had already been organizing against segregation in

Montgomery for years. For numerous accounts of the boycott and its effects in launching the modern Black freedom movement, see Jeanne Theoharis, *The Rebellious Life of Mrs. Rosa Parks* (Boston: Beacon Press, 2013).

3. SCLC consisted of a network of courageous Black ministers such as those mentioned by Rev. Lawson; Rev. Shuttlesworth was perhaps the bravest of them all. See Andrew Manis, *A Fire You Can't Put Out: The Civil Rights Life of Birmingham's Reverend Fred Shuttlesworth* (Tuscaloosa: University of Alabama Press, 1999). For references to individuals and history mentioned by Rev. Lawson, see the resources offered by the Martin Luther King Jr. Research and Education Institute at Stanford University, https://kinginstitute.stanford.edu/.

4. SNCC workers across the South played a key role in the southern movement. See Clayborn Carson, *In Struggle: SNCC and the Black Awakening of the 1960s* (Cambridge, MA: Harvard University Press, 1981). Cordell Reagon later became a member of the SNCC Freedom Singers. Music and religion combined as a powerful force in the movement. See Pete Seeger and Bob Reiser, *Everybody Says Freedom* (New York: W.W. Norton, 1989); Guy and Candy Carawan, *Freedom Is a Constant Struggle* (New York: Oak Publications, 1968); and *Sing for Freedom: The Story of the Civil Rights Movement through Its Songs* (Montgomery, AL: NewSouth Books, 2008). See also John Lewis, *Walking with the Wind: A Memoir of the Movement,* with Mike D'Orso (New York: Simon and Schuster, 1998).

7. A Brief Biography of James M. Lawson Jr.

1. James M. Lawson Jr., personal interview with Michael K. Honey, February 26, 2008, Tacoma, Washington. See also Dennis Dickerson, "James M. Lawson, Jr.: Methodism, Nonviolence, and the Civil Rights Movement," *Methodist History* 52, no. 3 (April 2014): 168–86.

2. James M. Lawson Jr., in discussion with Kent Wong and Kelly Lytle Hernandez, Spring 2013, Los Angeles.

3. Peter Ackerman and Jack DuVall, *A Force More Powerful: A Century of Nonviolent Conflict* (New York: St. Martin's Press, 2000), 308; James M. Lawson Jr., interview with Preeti Sharma and Ana Luz González, July 7, 2014, Los Angeles.

4. Ackerman and DuVall, *Force More Powerful,* 307. Muste was a powerful force in the peace, labor, and freedom movements from the 1920s through the

1960s. See Leilah Danielson, *American Gandhi: A. J. Muste and the History of Radicalism in the Twentieth Century* (Philadelphia: University of Pennsylvania Press, 2014).

5. The Freedom Rides were conceived by members of FOR and CORE, which was founded in 1942. See Congress of Racial Equality, "The History of CORE," CORE website, http://www.core-online.org/History/history.htm; Raymond Arsenault, *Freedom Riders: 1961 and the Struggle for Racial Justice* (New York: Oxford University Press, 2006).

6. Lawson, interview by Sharma and González.

7. Ernest M. Limbo, "James Lawson: The Nashville Civil Rights Movement," in *The Human Tradition in the Civil Rights Movement,* edited by Susan M. Glisson, chapter 8 (Lanham, MD: Rowman and Littlefield, 2006), 163.

8. Part 1, *A Force More Powerful: A Century of Nonviolent Conflict,* produced and directed by Steve York, 1999, https://www.nonviolent-conflict.org/force-powerful-english/.

9. Lawson, discussion with Wong and Lytle Hernandez.

10. Limbo, "James Lawson," 162.

11. The *Nagpur Times* was a daily newspaper printed in English. Lawson states that it provided consistent coverage on Martin Luther King Jr. and the Montgomery bus boycotts. Lawson, interview by Sharma and González.

12. For an overview of how James Lawson came to nonviolence and began to teach it in the South, see David Halberstam, *The Children* (New York: Ballantine, 1999), chapters 1–3.

13. See Limbo, "James Lawson," 163.

14. David M. Oshinsky, "Freedom Riders," *New York Times,* March 15, 1998, https://www.nytimes.com/1998/03/15/books/freedom-riders.html

15. For information on the early Nashville nonviolence workshops and various people and actions involved in the movement, see Halberstam, *The Children,* chapters 4–6.

16. Theo Emery, "Activist Ousted from Vanderbilt Is Back, as a Teacher," *New York Times,* October 4, 2006, http://www.nytimes.com/2006/10/04/education/04lawson.html.

17. Ackerman and DuVall, *A Force More Powerful,* 323; United Press International, "Divinity Dean Out in Racial Protest: Vanderbilt University Aide Resigns over Refusal to Readmit Negro Student," *New York Times,* May 31, 1960. See

also Limbo, "James Lawson," 171–73; Clayborne Carson, *In Struggle: SNCC and the Black Awakening of the 1960s* (Cambridge, MA: Harvard University Press, 1995); Halberstam, *The Children.*

18. "Negroes Press Protest in South, but the Cold Limits Activities," *New York Times,* March 4, 1960.

19. Howard Zinn, *SNCC: The New Abolitionists* (Boston: Beacon Press, 1964), 33. Halberstam, *The Children,* chapter 38. Women played a crucial role in SNCC. Diane Nash gives her own account in Faith S. Holsaert, Martha Prescod Norman Noonan, Judy Richardson, Betty Garmon Robinson, Jean Smith Young, and Dorothy M. Zellner, eds., *Hands on the Plow: Personal Accounts by Women in SNCC* (Champaign: University of Illinois Press, 2010), 77–83. See also Mary King, *Freedom Song* (New York: William Morrow and Company, 1987).

20. Zinn, *SNCC,* 51. For more information about Diane Nash's coordinating role, see Jennifer A. Stollman, "Diane Nash: 'Courage Displaces Fear, Love Transforms Hate': Civil Rights Activism and the Commitment to Nonviolence," in *The Human Tradition in the Civil Rights Movement,* edited by Susan M. Glisson, chapter 10 (Lanham, MD: Rowman and Littlefield, 2006), 163. See also Arsenault, *Freedom Riders*; and David M. Oshinsky, *Worse Than Slavery: Parchman Farm and the Ordeal of Jim Crow Justice* (New York: Free Press, 1997).

21. The name of the church was changed in 1968 to Centenary United Methodist Church.

22. Michael K. Honey, *Going Down Jericho Road: The Memphis Strike, Martin Luther King's Last Campaign* (New York: W. W. Norton, 2007), 203. See also Ben Kamin, *Room 306: The National Story of the Lorraine Motel* (East Lansing: Michigan State University Press, 2012), 46.

23. Lawson explains that at this time African American ministers formed Community on the Move for Equality (COME) to continue to advocate for sanitation workers; the organization was funded from money raised for the strike fund. James M. Lawson Jr., interview by Preeti Sharma and Ana Luz González, September 4, 2014, Los Angeles. For more details, see Honey, *Going Down Jericho Road,* chapter 10.

24. Martin Luther Jr., "I've Been to the Mountaintop," speech, Memphis, April 3, 1968, King Papers, Martin Luther King Jr. Research and Education Institute, Stanford University, http://mlk-kpp01.stanford.edu/index.php /encyclopedia/documentsentry/ive_been_to_the_mountaintop.

25. Honey, *Going Down Jericho Road,* epilogue.

26. Lawson, interview by Sharma and González, September 4, 2014.

27. See Helene Slessarev-Jamir, *Prophetic Activism: Progressive Religious Justice Movements in Contemporary America* (New York: New York University Press, 2011), 109; and Pierrette Hondagneu-Sotelo, *God's Heart Has No Borders: How Religious Activists Are Working for Immigrant Rights* (Berkeley: University of California Press, 2008), 88.

28. Lawson, interview by Sharma and González, September 4, 2014.

29. James M. Lawson Jr., "The Uplift of All: Gandhi, King, and the Global Struggle for Freedom and Justice Conference," with Mary Elizabeth King, Stanford University, October 12, 2019.

For more about the Gandhi-King Global Initiative and King's vision at the World House Project, Stanford, see https://cddrl.fsi.stanford.edu/world-house /world-house-project-main-page. For nonviolence lesson plans, check out the Liberation Curriculum, https://cddrl.fsi.stanford.edu/world-house/resources /liberation-curriculum, and https://kinginstitute.stanford.edu/liberation-curriculum/lesson-plans/activities/kings-world-house. For details on the James Lawson Institute and Mary Elizabeth King, see https://jameslawsoninstitute .org/history/. For more than two decades, James Lawson has taught a course on nonviolence and social movements at the UCLA Labor Center, inspiring a new generation of young activists. In 2018, James Lawson was awarded the UCLA Medal, its highest honor. In 2021, the California State Legislature allocated $15 million to establish a permanent home for the UCLA Labor Center that has been named the UCLA James Lawson Jr. Worker Justice Center. For more information, see https://www.labor.ucla.edu/about/overview/. See also the Martin Luther King, Jr., Center for Nonviolent Social Change, https:// thekingcenter.org; and the National Civil Rights Museum, on the Memphis sanitation strike and James Lawson, https://www.civilrightsmuseum.org/i-am-a-man.

Contributing Authors

Rev. Lawson with University of Washington, Tacoma, Black Student Union leader Patricia George, Michael K. Honey, and University of Washington, Tacoma, Black Student Union leader Will Johnson.

MICHAEL K. HONEY is Haley Professor of Humanities at the University of Washington, Tacoma, the author of five award-winning labor and freedom movement studies and oral histories, and editor of King's labor speeches, *All Labor Has Dignity* (2011). His most recent book is *To the Promised Land: Martin Luther King and the Fight for Economic Justice* (2019). His *Going Down Jericho Road: The Memphis Strike, Martin Luther King's Last Campaign* (2007) won the Robert F. Kennedy Book Award and other national awards. He has been a Guggenheim and Radcliffe Institute fellow, the Harry Bridges Chair of Labor Studies at the University of Washington, president of the Labor and Working-Class History Association, and a southern organizer, filmmaker, and musician.

Rev. Lawson and Kent Wong.

KENT WONG is the director of the UCLA Labor Center, where he has taught a course on nonviolence with Rev. James Lawson Jr. for the past twenty years. Previously, he served as staff attorney for the Service Employees International Union and the first staff attorney for Asian Americans Advancing Justice in Los Angeles. He was the founding president of the Asian Pacific American Labor Alliance, AFL-CIO, and has published more than a dozen books on the labor movement, immigrant rights, and the Asian American community.

Angela Davis. Photograph by K. K. Otteson.

ANGELA Y. DAVIS is a philosopher and an antiracist, feminist scholar and activist. As a former political prisoner, she is well known for her campaigns to abolish prisons, to free political prisoners, and to end repression and police violence. She has a distinguished academic career and has written numerous pathbreaking studies, including *Women, Race and Class* (1981), *Blues Legacies and Black Feminism* (1999), *Are Prisons Obsolete?* (2003), *Abolition Democracy* (2005), and *Freedom Is a Constant Struggle* (2015), among others. She is Distinguished Professor Emerita of the History of Consciousness and Feminist Studies at the University of California, Santa Cruz.

Bryan Stevenson. Courtesy of Equal Justice Initiative.

BRYAN STEVENSON is the founder of the Equal Justice Initiative and has won major legal cases before the US Supreme Court to challenge unfair and abusive treatment of the incarcerated. He has created nationally acclaimed cultural sites in Montgomery, Alabama, and is a professor at New York University School of Law. His book *Just Mercy: A Story of Justice and Redemption* (2014) has been made into a major motion picture and has helped to spur efforts to end the death penalty.